PRACTICE TESTS FOR CAMBRIDGE FIRST CERTIFICATE in ENGLISH

PRACTICE TESTS FOR

CAMBRIDGE

FIRST CERTIFICATE in ENGLISH

SET ONE

Margaret Archer   Enid Nolan-Woods

Nelson

Thomas Nelson and Sons Ltd
Nelson House Mayfield Road
Walton-on-Thames Surrey KT12 5PL

51 York Place
Edinburgh EH1 3JD

Yi Xiu Factory Building
Unit 05-06 5th Floor
65 Sims Avenue Singapore 1438

Thomas Nelson (Hong Kong) Ltd
Toppan Building 10/F
22A Westlands Road
Quarry Bay Hong Kong

Thomas Nelson (Kenya) Ltd
P.O. Box 18123
Nairobi Kenya

First published by Thomas Nelson and Sons Ltd 1983
Reprinted 1984

ISBN 0-17-555471-4

NCN 71-ECE 9156-02

Printed in Hong Kong

ACKNOWLEDGEMENTS

Thanks are due to the following for permission to reproduce copyright material:

Auberon Waugh and The Spectator for an extract from *Freedom from Bats;* Elliot Right Way Books for an extract from *A—Z of Do-It-Yourself In The Home* by Harold and Elizabeth King; Usborne Publishing Ltd. for the instructions for 'Battlezone' from *The Usborne Guide to Computer and Video Games;* Barclays Bank for their information leaflet on travellers' cheques and currency; Granada Publishing Ltd. for an extract from *Great Theatrical Disasters* by Gyles Brandreth.

Photographs by D. Lewcock

Design by Colin Lewis

Illustrations by MULTIPLEX techniques ltd.

Contents

Notes to the Student

The object of this book is to provide students preparing for the University of Cambridge First Certificate in English with complete practice in the Written and Oral papers. Each of the five tests consists of three written and two oral papers as follows:

WRITTEN PAPERS

Paper 1 Reading Comprehension (1 hour)

Section A Twenty-five multiple choice questions testing vocabulary and formal grammatical control, in sentence contexts.
Section B Fifteen multiple choice reading comprehension questions based on three or more texts, which may include information in graphic form, designed to test comprehension of gist or detailed content.

Paper 2 Composition (1½ hours)

Two compositions from a choice of descriptive, narrative or discursive topics, or topics based on prescribed reading.
Assessment will be based on organisation and clarity of content, accuracy of grammatical control, fluency and range of expression.

Paper 3 Use of English (2 hours)

Section A Open-completion or transformation items designed to test active control of the language.
Section B Directed writing exercise to test ability to interpret and present information.

ORAL PAPERS

Paper 4 Listening Comprehension (approx. 30 minutes)

Questions of varying type (selection, re-ordering, blank-filling etc.) to test accurate understanding of spoken English, based on recorded material including conversation, announcements etc.

Paper 5 Interview (approx. 20 minutes)

(i) Conversation on a picture stimulus, assessed on fluency and grammatical accuracy.
(ii) Reading aloud of a short passage (announcement, instruction or situation), assessed on pronunciation of individual sounds and on stress and linking in phrases.
(iii) Structured communication exercise (role-play, discussion etc. on prescribed texts or unprepared material), assessed on communicative ability and vocabulary.

A Teacher's Edition of this Book is available, with Answers.

Cassettes of the Listening Comprehension material for Paper 4 are available. The passages for reading aloud from Paper 5 are also included.

Test One

PAPER 1 READING COMPREHENSION (1 hour)

SECTION A

In this section you must choose the word or phrase which best completes each sentence. Indicate the letter A, B, C or D against the number of each item 1 to 25 for the word or phrase you choose. ***Give one answer only*** *to each question.*

1 The .... from the gate to the cottage was overgrown with weeds.
A road B street C path D passage

2 The field was surrounded by .... wire.
A spiked B barbed C pricked D scratched

3 He has just been .... to Senior Clerk.
A promoted B raised C elevated D advanced

4 The football match resulted in a ....
A loss B equaliser C draw D zero

5 Paul Black is .... as Labour MP for Brightford in the next election.
A sitting B standing C presenting D appearing

6 My boss insists on seeing everything in .... before he makes a decision.
A red, white and blue B green and yellow C black and white
D black and blue

7 How .... is it from here to the city centre?
A long B far C distant D near

8 I don't understand why people put .... with the bad service in this restaurant.
A upon B over C up D down

9 Do you think there's any .... of him passing the exam?
A chance B opportunity C occasion D expectancy

10 Our school doesn't break .... until the end of July.
A out B in C off D up

11 When he was studying he stayed at a student .... in London.
A hospital B house C hostel D hotel

12 Do .... if you come to London.
A look me up B find me out C take me up D show me up

13 The .... from the explosion broke every window in the street.
A force B bang C blast D draught

14 To .... the truth I don't really understand computers.
A say B allow C admit D tell

15 I had to have two .... when I went to the dentist last week.
A fillings B refills C filings D paddings

16 Mrs Jones has offered a .... for the return of her lost cat.
A prize B bonus C tip D reward

17 I phoned him this morning but when I said who I was he ....
A rang up B hung up C shut down D shut up

18 Pass me the salad .... please.
A sauce B seasoning C spice D dressing

19 You'll find his number in the telephone ....
A directory B index C catalogue D list

20 Those prawns we had for supper have given me ....
A indisposition B infection C sickness D indigestion

21 I don't think he's the sort of man who will ever .... much money.
A acquire B gain C obtain D make

22 He's .... First Certificate next June.
A passing B taking C attending D making

23 We were the .... students in the class who could speak Spanish.
A one B single C only D alone

24 What are you going to do when you .... school?
A conclude B end C complete D leave

25 When he died he left .... amounting to £50,000.
A accounts B debts C obligations D payments

SECTION B

In this section you will find after each of the passages a number of questions or unfinished statements about the passage, each with four suggested answers or ways of finishing. You must choose the one which you think fits best. Underline the letter A, B, C or D against the number of each item, 26 to 40, for the answer you choose. ***Give one answer only*** *to each question. Read each passage right through before choosing your answers.*

FIRST PASSAGE

Package holidays, covering a two weeks' stay in an attractive location are increasingly popular, because they offer an inclusive price with few extras. Once you get to the airport, it is up to the tour operator to see that you get safely to your destination. Excursions, local entertainment, swimming, sunbathing, skiing—you name it—it's all laid on for you. There is, in fact, no reason for you to bother to arrange anything yourselves. You make friends and have a good time, but there is very little chance that you will really get to know the local people. This is even less likely on a coach tour, when you spend almost your entire time travelling. Of course, there are carefully scheduled stops for you to visit historic buildings and monuments, but you will probably be allowed only a brief stay overnight in some famous city, with a polite reminder to be up and breakfasted early in time for the coach next morning. You may visit the beautiful, the historic, the ancient, but time is always at your elbow. There is also the added disadvantage of being obliged to spend your holiday with a group of people you have never met before, may not like and have no reasonable excuse for getting away from. As against this, it can be argued that for many people, particularly the lonely or elderly, the feeling of belonging to a group, albeit for a short period on holiday, is an added bonus. They can sit safely back in their seats and watch the world go by.

26 When you go on a package holiday

A there are not many additional charges.

B there is no charge for extras.

C flight times are arranged by the tour operator.

D your safe arrival is ensured.

27 The kind of people who go on these holidays

A are too lazy to amuse themselves.

B expect the tour operator to amuse them.

C find most of their interests catered for.

D have no contact with the local people.

28 On a coach tour it is often exhausting, because you

A are so highly organised.
B are constantly on the move.
C don't like the other people on the tour.
D don't get enough sleep.

29 For some people, travelling in an organised group

A provides a sense of security.
B is their only opportunity to make friends.
C is the only way they can get about.
D helps them to understand themselves better.

SECOND PASSAGE

Voluntary Service Overseas (VSO) is a registered charity dedicated to assisting development in the world's poor countries. It is an independent non-sectarian organisation. VSO is a direct response to an urgent need. Each year about 450 volunteers are sent to work on projects in 36 developing countries. Each volunteer goes overseas in response to a specific appeal from a developing country. Over the past 23 years more than 20,000 volunteers have worked abroad with VSO. Together they have contributed over 30,000 man-years to development.

But VSO volunteers gain as well as give. They gain responsibility, experience and a personal viewpoint on development. On their return they can make an effective contribution to the development debate. Above all, VSO is aid that the Third World needs. For this reason the Third World countries themselves pay almost half the cost of each VSO volunteer.

When VSO was established over 20 years ago, the first volunteers were school-leavers. However, increasingly the demand was for skilled and professional people. Today, all VSO volunteers are skilled and/or qualified people—teachers and doctors, mechanics and electricians, accountants and civil engineers. Why do they volunteer? To make a personal contribution, to take on extra responsibility, to gain overseas work experience, to work within a community—often for all these reasons. The task of VSO is to match these specialists with particular vacancies, notified to them by overseas countries. Then, having made the match, they prepare the volunteer to work for two years in a very different environment.

30 The work of VSO is concerned with

A helping the poor in all parts of the world.
B giving practical assistance to poor countries.
C the development of any worthwhile project.
D increasing the need for development in the Third World.

31 To date the number of volunteers who have worked for VSO is

A in excess of 23,000.

B more than 30,000.

C over 20,000.

D about 450.

32 The experience gained by VSO volunteers working abroad

A provides the basic training they need.

B increases their understanding of particular problems.

C helps them to deal with their own problems.

D encourages them to contribute to Third World appeals.

33 The majority of VSO volunteers today are

A over-qualified.

B unskilled.

C school-leavers.

D highly trained.

34 People who volunteer for VSO do so

A for a variety of reasons.

B because they have personal problems.

C in response to requests from overseas.

D because they are unemployed.

35 A volunteer who is accepted must be prepared to

A take a two-year training course.

B be away from home for two years.

C spend two years visiting different countries.

D take two years to adapt to a new environment.

THIRD PASSAGE

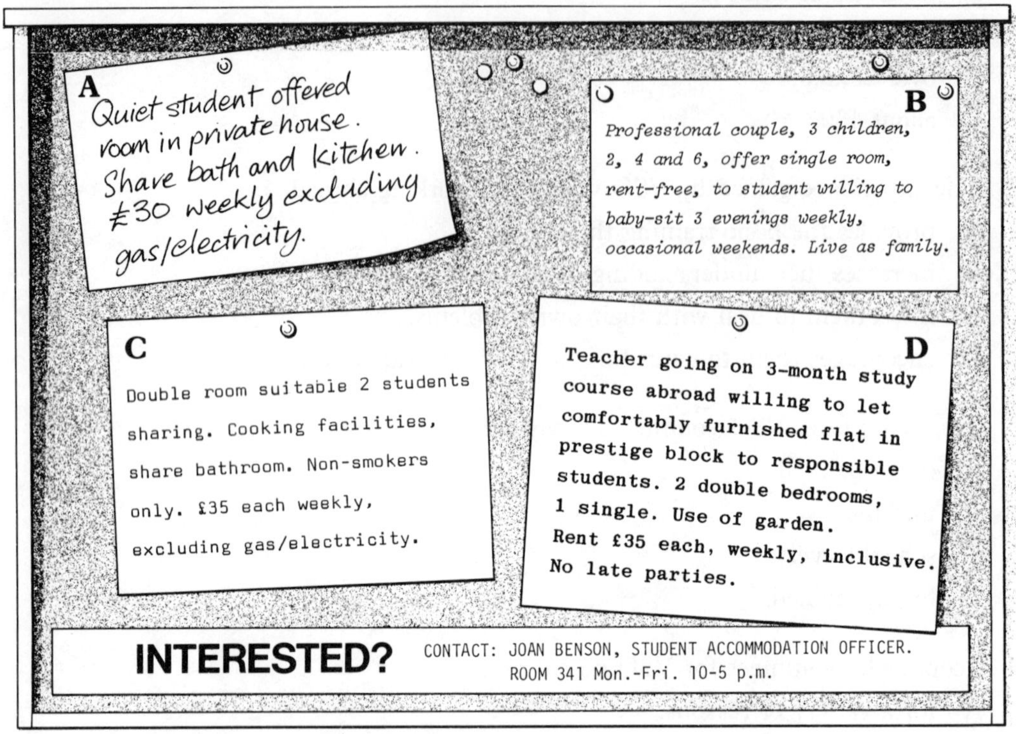
A
Quiet student offered room in private house. Share bath and kitchen. £30 weekly excluding gas/electricity.
B
Professional couple, 3 children, 2, 4 and 6, offer single room, rent-free, to student willing to baby-sit 3 evenings weekly, occasional weekends. Live as family.
C
Double room suitable 2 students sharing. Cooking facilities, share bathroom. Non-smokers only. £35 each weekly, excluding gas/electricity.
D
Teacher going on 3-month study course abroad willing to let comfortably furnished flat in prestige block to responsible students. 2 double bedrooms, 1 single. Use of garden. Rent £35 each, weekly, inclusive. No late parties.
INTERESTED?
CONTACT: JOAN BENSON, STUDENT ACCOMMODATION OFFICER.
ROOM 341 Mon.-Fri. 10-5 p.m.

36 This information comes from

A an advertisement in a newspaper.

B a notice in the window of an estate agent.

C a college notice board.

D a leaflet distributed by students.

37 The single room offered in **A** would be suitable for a student

A in need of relaxation.

B doing intensive study.

C anxious to make new friends.

D wanting self-contained accommodation.

38 A student accepting the offer in **B**

A must have had experience of child care.

B would have no free time.

C must be a member of a large family.

D would be able to live very cheaply.

39 For two students **D** would be more economical than **C** because

A they would share a room.

B the basic expenses are cheaper.

C there are no extras except for food.

D there is free use of the garden.

40 The flat offered in **D** is ____________

A only available for a short period.

B is on the first floor.

C can only accommodate four people.

D is expensively furnished.

PAPER 2 COMPOSITION (1½ hours)

Write ***two only*** *of the following composition exercises. Your answers must follow exactly the instructions given, and must be of between 120 and 180 words each.*

1 Write a letter to the chairman of your local council complaining about the poor lighting in your street and the hazards it causes. You should make the beginning and the ending like those of an ordinary letter, but the address is not to be counted in the number of words.

2 You have witnessed an accident in which a motorcyclist was hit by a car and seriously injured. Write an account of what happened.

3 Describe any food that is a speciality of your country and how and when it is served.

4 The influence of TV on young children.

5 (See Appendix: Prescribed texts)

PAPER 3 USE OF ENGLISH (2 hours)

SECTION A

1 *Fill each of the numbered blanks in the following passage. Use only* **one** *word in each space.*

There are people who .... (1) they are not influenced .... (2) advertisements. They buy only .... (3) they want to buy and they know what they .... (4). Usually, however, they buy goods that are familiar .... (5) them because the brand .... (6) have appeared .... (7) often in newspaper advertisements and television commercials .... (8) they recognise them immediately when they see them on the .... (9) of the supermarket. Shoppers are slow to change their habits and it .... (10) a long and persistent campaign on the part of the advertiser to .... (11) them that a new product is .... (12) trying. Possibly the easiest products to sell are .... (13) which claim to alter our physical .... (14). Most of us dream of .... (15) more attractive, stronger and healthier than we .... (16). If .... (17) we had the self-confidence of the people we see smiling at us from advertisements, all our problems would be .... (18), or at .... (19) so we tell ourselves. We only half believe it, but we go out and buy the product all the .... (20).

2 *Finish each of the following sentences in such a way that it means exactly the same as the sentence printed before it.*

EXAMPLE: Do you want any more coffee?

ANSWER: Would you *like some more coffee?*

a) Joan and I attended the same school.
Joan and I were ....

b) No one ever uses this room.
This room ....

c) Who owns that sports car?
Who does ....

d) This building is said to be 2,000 years old.
They ....

e) What about going to the cinema tonight?
Why ……………………………………………………………………

f) Is this the right way to the station?
Am I ……………………………………………………………………

g) I'm too busy to talk to you now.
I haven't ……………………………………………………………………

h) He always gets to work on time.
He's ……………………………………………………………………

i) I tried to lift the box but it was too heavy.
The box ……………………………………………………………………

j) I'm sorry to have kept you waiting.
I must ……………………………………………………………………

3 *Write in the space in each of the following sentences the correct phrase made from LOOK.*

EXAMPLE: He went to *look over* the flat.

a) Aunt Mary ………… the children when their mother died.

b) I ………… for a flat for six months now.

c) Don't wait for me. I want to have ………… the cathedral.

d) The committee promised that they ………… the matter.

4 *Write in the space in each of the following sentences the correct word or phrase containing BACK.*

EXAMPLE: After the show was over he went *backstage* to talk to some of the performers.

a) Don't walk ………… or you'll fall in the swimming pool.

b) This is a picture of the beach but you can just see our hotel in the ………… .

c) Paul was going to come to the meeting with us, but he ………… at the last moment.

d) I hope you don't mind my saying so, but I think you've got your sweater on ………… .

5 *Make all the changes and additions necessary to produce, from the following eight sets of words and phrases, eight sentences which together make a complete letter. Note carefully from the example what kind of alterations need to be made. Write each sentence in the space provided.*

EXAMPLE: I/hope/he/give/careful consideration/my application.

ANSWER: *I hope he will give careful consideration to my application.*

Dear Sir,

I/write/reply/your advertisement/position chief accountant/Manchester branch.

a) ....

I/be/qualified accountant and/work/Smith and Brown, Architects/last four years.

b) ....

They/be happy/give/you/reference.

c) ....

I/be anxious/improve/my position/as/have/wife/two children/support.

d) ....

I/be glad/opportunity/take on/more responsibility.

e) ....

We/be willing/move/London/Manchester/short notice.

f) ....

I/be happy/present job/but/no prospects/promotion.

g) ....

I/hope/hear/you/earliest convenience.

h) ....

Yours faithfully,

James Greene

SECTION B

6 *Using the information given in the following conversation, continue each of the four paragraphs in the spaces provided. Use about 50 words for each paragraph.*

CAROLINE: You know, the trouble with this firm is that there are too many bosses and too few workers.

GEORGE: What do you mean? We're all workers.

CAROLINE: No, we're not. We're bosses. I'm in charge of Personnel and you're Sales Manager. I engage staff and try to sort out their personal problems and generally keep them happy, but I don't go looking for them. I wait for them to come to me. I don't go down and work on the factory floor myself. Everything I deal with—aggression, individualism, racial prejudice—is secondhand.

GEORGE: Yes, but surely that's the whole idea. You have to be objective. You wouldn't be able to give them the right advice if you were mixed up in all their problems.

CAROLINE: Of course I would. I'd be one of them. I'd be able to judge much better if they were telling me their troubles, or if they were just having me on because they'd had a row with someone or thought the foreman had a down on them—things like that. As for you ...

GEORGE: What about me?

CAROLINE: Well, all you deal with are facts and figures, not people. You don't have to go out on the road and try to get orders from people you don't like and spend most of your nights in second-rate hotels up and down the country.

GEORGE: Most of our reps do a pretty good job. Sales figures have been most encouraging this year. I admit there are one or two areas where I think we could do better.

CAROLINE: That's exactly what I mean. 'You think'—you don't know. You sit there in your comfortable office with your three telephones and you can make or break a man just by looking at a sales chart. You're a boss. You don't do the real work, but you're paid twice as much as the people who do.

GEORGE: Aren't you getting things a bit out of proportion? Any organisation needs managers and managers need the workers. So long as there's a good relationship between them the firm will prosper.

CAROLINE: Oh, it's all too easy from where you and I are standing. I think every boss should spend at least three months every year working on the factory floor, subject to the same rules and discipline as all the other workers.

GEORGE: Would you be prepared to do that yourself?

CAROLINE: In theory, yes, but in practice, no. I haven't got any practical skills, you see, so I don't think I'd be a lot of use. I'd probably always be running to the Personnel Office to try and get myself moved to another department.

Caroline says that everything she deals with is secondhand because ....

....

....

....

....

George thinks the role of a Personnel Officer ....

....

....

....

....

....

In Caroline's opinion, the Sales Manager ....

....

....

....

....

....

Caroline has to admit that, in practice, her ideas ....

....

....

....

....

....

PAPER 4 LISTENING COMPREHENSION (Approx. 30 minutes)

FIRST PART

Fill in the information you hear on the form below. Some of it has been filled in for you.

USER ORDER FORM

PHONE SOCKETS (✓number required)

1–5	6–10	11–15	16–20	21+

RADIO PAGING (35p a day): **NATURE OF BUSINESS USE**

Salesman/ contact

ELECTRONIC BUSINESS SYSTEMS (✓system required)

MONARCH 120		PREMIERE		HERALD	
GREY	BROWN	GREY	BROWN	GREY	BROWN

Person Contacted . . . .

Office use only

Name . . . .

Job Title PA to Managing Director

COMPANY NAME (Please print one letter in each box)

N E O F A X A L T D

ADDRESS

TELEPHONE NUMBER

Company's line of business . . . .

Number of employees . . . .

Signature J. Browning.

Date . . . .

Date convenient for installation . . . .

SECOND PART

For each of the questions 1—4 put a tick (✓) in one of the boxes A, B, C or D.

1 Mr Harper telephoned Briggs and Broom because he

A had forgotten an appointment.
B had been caught in the traffic.
C wanted to alter an arrangement.
D couldn't see Mr Briggs that day.

A	
B	
C	
D	

2 Mr Briggs's secretary

A told Mr Harper to ring back later.
B promised to get in touch with him.
C asked him to dictate a message.
D agreed to change the appointment.

A	
B	
C	
D	

3 When Mr Briggs returned, his secretary told him Mr Harper

A had changed his appointment.
B was coming at a different time.
C would be unable to see him.
D had been delayed.

A	
B	
C	
D	

4 Mr Harper and Mr Briggs arranged

A to discuss business over lunch.
B to lunch in the office.
C to have a meal out.
D to meet at 2.30.

A	
B	
C	
D	

⟨ He objected that his secretary was late in work.

wish ~~not missed~~
x I ~~wish not missed~~ myself to ~~not~~ didn't miss your birthday party

x The streets were dirty this week.
The streets haven't been cleaned ...

~~Apples are not~~ as expensive as oranges.

~~It is such a dirty restaurant~~

~~He~~ objected TO his secretary BEING late.

I wish I hadn't missed ...
I wish I could have come to your ...
It is such no one wants eat, ~~the~~ because the restaurant is dirty

Altenation of generation life cycle.

meiosis.

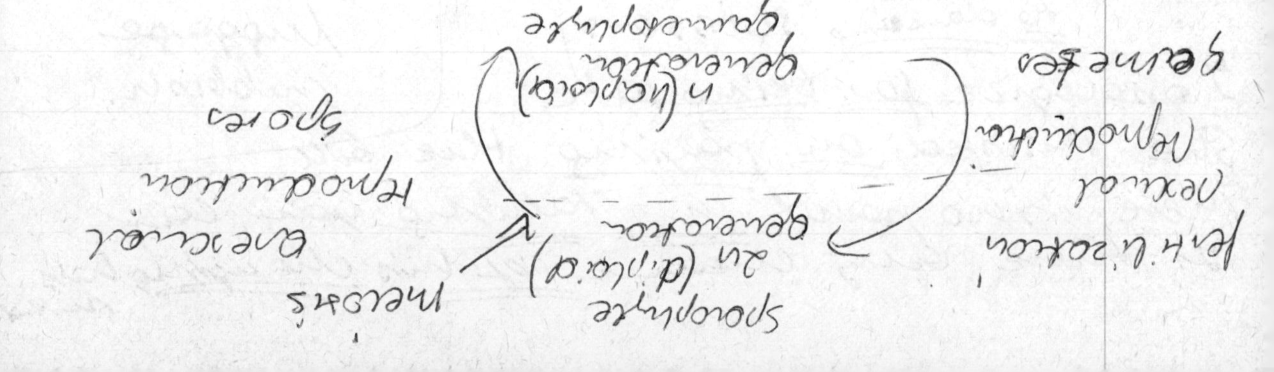

~~[illegible]~~

Shorthand Typist. 12 w. ~~5/88~~ 504

S audio typist. 14 w ~~5/88~~ 588

~~Shorthand~~ Audio-Typist 10 420

Have you any objection to changing your working hours

I'm in favour of giving everyone a day off

8-4.30 Did you have any difficulty in finding the house.

15 Forth Street Edinburgh

In spite of having no qualifications he got the job.

Name Mr. [illegible]. ~~[illegible]~~. Lewis

Adress 27 ABB~~EY~~ Rd London. N11

Philips Words which are always plural

H

plural	Singular
people.	news
police	furniture
cloth	advice
pyjames	knowledge
glasses	luggage
scissors	rubbish.

He left without paying

He prefers drinking to dancing

I apologize for being late

She insisted on paying the bill

There is no point in taking your car

Is there any chance of his changing his mind.

PAPER 2 COMPOSITION (1½ hours)

*Write **two only** of the following composition exercises. Your answers must follow exactly the instructions given, and must be of between 120 and 180 words each.*

1 Write a letter to somebody thanking him/her for an invitation to a party but explaining why you are unable to attend. You should make the beginning and the ending like those of an ordinary letter, but the address is not to be counted in the number of words.

2 Your best friend has just got engaged. Write the speech of congratulation you would give at the engagement party.

3 Write an account of your visit to a foreign country that you had never visited before.

4 What are the advantages and disadvantages of the motor car?

5 (See Appendix: Prescribed texts)

PAPER 3 USE OF ENGLISH (2 hours)

SECTION A

1 *Fill each of the numbered blanks in the following passage. Use only **one** word in each space.*

Ever .... (1) she was a child Milada had wanted to visit America. She had heard .... (2) much about it; the tall, glittering skyscrapers, the teeming streets and the restless excitement of New York. .... (3), she was here. But it was .... (4) so different from what she had expected. It was .... (5) the streets were bustling with life but they were .... (6) exceedingly noisy; the people were not very polite .... (7) but pushed and jostled her unceasingly. So, after a .... (8) while she turned with relief into the peace and .... (9) of Central Park. Wandering along in the sunshine, she .... (10) recovered her good humour and decided to .... (11) the Museum of Modern Art. Not being .... (12) where it was she consulted her city guide but discovered the .... (13) page was missing. Looking .... (14) for someone to ask, she found that she was all .... (15) in the park. Visions of muggers jumping out .... (16) behind bushes flashed through her .... (17) so she started to walk faster .... (18) the park gate. .... (19) as she was approaching it, she heard a sound behind her, but turning, found it was only a branch .... (20) from a tree.

2 *Finish each of the following sentences in such a way that it means exactly the same as the sentence printed before it.*

EXAMPLE: He went out in spite of the rain.

ANSWER: Although *it was raining, he still went out.*

a) The bus strike prevented me from going to work.
I wasn't ....

b) He didn't know enough English to pass the examination.
He found the English examination ....

c) Is it possible to get to Paris from here?
I wonder ....

d) If I had seen him, I wouldn't have gone home.
As I didn't ....

e) I have never eaten a better meal.
That ....

f) How much is that jacket in the window?
What ....

g) The teacher made the class stay in after school.
The class ....

h) Let's try that new restaurant that's just opened.
How ....

i) I started going to Scotland for my holidays five years ago.
I have ....

j) For the first time he knew the meaning of happiness.
He had never ....

3 *Write in the space in each of the following sentences the correct phrase made from TAKE.*

EXAMPLE: The policeman *took down* details of the accident.

a) Last year she .... much more work than she could manage.

b) Sorry, you're right. I .... what I said.

c) Looking at him closely, I can see he .... his mother.

d) That company will .... by a multi-national soon.

e) I was .... by the news of the wedding. It was such a shock.

f) He was a very skilled confidence trickster, everyone was .... by him.

g) Since she has been made redundant, she has been forced .... needlework.

h) The plane .... at seven o'clock in the morning.

4 *Make all the changes and additions necessary to produce, from the following eight sets of words and phrases, eight sentences which together make a complete letter. Note carefully from the example what kind of alterations need to be made. Write each sentence in the space provided.*

EXAMPLE: I/hope/receive/reply/letter/before now.

ANSWER: *I was hoping to receive a reply to my letter before now.*

Dear Sir,

I write/complain/electric toaster/I buy/your store.

a) ....

When/I get/home/unpack/find/chrome/be chipped.

b) ....

That/not be all/when/I plug in/toaster/switch on/nothing happen.

c) ....

I check/plug/discover/fuse go/so/put in/new one .

d) ....

This time/toaster/work/so I try/make/toast.

e) ....

first piece/not do/but/stay/white/highest setting.

f) ....

next piece/turn/black/lowest setting.

g) ....

I be please/you exchange/this toaster/refund/money.

h) ....

Yours faithfully,

James Brown

SECTION B

5 *Using the information given in the following article, continue each of the four paragraphs in the spaces provided. Use about 50 words for each paragraph.*

Computer people talk a lot about the need for other people to become 'computer-literate', in other words, to learn to understand computers and what makes them tick. But not all experts agree, however, that this is a good idea.

One pioneer, in particular, who disagrees is David Tebbutt, the founder of Computertown UK. Although many people see this as a successful attempt to bring people closer to the computer, David does not see it that way. He says that Computertown UK was formed for just the opposite reason, to bring computers to the people and make them 'people-literate'.

David first got the idea when he visited one of America's best-known computer 'guru' figures, Bob Albrecht, in the small university town of Palo Alto in Northern California. Albrecht had started a project called Computertown USA in the local library, and the local children used to call round every Wednesday to borrow some time on the computers there, instead of borrowing library books. Albrecht was always on hand to answer any questions and to help the children discover about computers in their own way.

Over here, in Britain, Computertowns have taken off in a big way, and there are now about 40 scattered over the country. David Tebbutt thinks they are most successful when tied to a computer club. He insists there is a vast and important difference between the two, although they complement each other. The clubs cater for the enthusiasts, with some computer knowledge already, who get together and eventually form an expert computer group. This frightens away non-experts, known as 'grockles', who are happier going to Computertowns where there are computers available for them to experiment on, with experts available to encourage them and answer any questions; they are not told what to do, they find out.

David Tebbutt finds it interesting to see the two different approaches working side by side. The computer experts have to learn not to tell people about computers, but have to be able to explain the answers to the questions that people really want to know. In some Computertowns there are question sessions, rather like radio phone-ins, where the experts listen to a lot of questons and then try to work out some structure to answer them. People are not having to learn computer jargon, but the experts are having to translate computer mysteries into easily understood terms; the computers are becoming 'people-literate'.

David Tebbutt disagrees with many people's concept of Computertown UK because...

....

....

....

....

....

In America, Bob Albrecht, a well-known computer expert tried out his ideas...

....

....

....

....

....

In Britain, people had found many disadvantages in computer clubs...

....

....

....

....

....

But they found a lot of advantages in the Computertowns...

....

....

....

....

....

PAPER 4 LISTENING COMPREHENSION (Approx. 30 minutes)

FIRST PART

For each of the questions 1—6 put a tick (✓) in one of the boxes A, B, C or D.

1 Why has Anne Frazer chosen *Spies Don't Cry* as the best espionage book of the year?

A It has a very complicated plot.
B The plot is very well worked out.
C It is the best of Johnson's books.
D It is the least disappointing of his books.

A	
B	
C	
D	

2 What is it that Frank Kelly doesn't like about *Spies Don't Cry*?

A It wasn't exciting enough.
B The characters died too easily.
C The thin characterisation.
D The plot wasn't developed very well.

A	
B	
C	
D	

3 The name of Brent Walker was introduced into the conversation to

A show how popular he is.
B prove that he was just a puppet.
C mention he has a fan club.
D indicate he has a well-rounded character.

A	
B	
C	
D	

4 The publishing companies

A charge high prices for long books.
B sell short books cheaply.
C trade on well-known authors' names.
D only increase the prices of recent books.

A	
B	
C	
D	

5 The other three books were rejected as Top Spy Book of the Year because they

A were too long.
B were too expensive.
C weren't long enough.
D weren't good enough.

A	
B	
C	
D	

6 What would probably be the result of choosing *Spies Don't Cry*?

A People would buy more copies.
B Publishers would put up prices.
C Authors would write more books.
D There would be more book programmes.

A	
B	
C	
D	

SECOND PART

For each of the questions 1—6 fill in the information in the boxes on the programme schedule. Number 1 has been done for you.

VISIT TO EXHIBITION

1	Train departs	9.00
2	Breakfast starts	
3	They arrive	
4	Exhibition opens	
5	Return train leaves	
6	They arrive back	

For each of the questions 7—9 put a tick (✓) in one of the boxes A, B, C or D.

7 Where do they decide to eat lunch?

A In the buffet car on the train.
B At the Red Lion pub.
C In the hotel restaurant.
D At a restaurant in the town.

A	
B	
C	
D	

8 They could expect to pay £11.50 for

A breakfast on the train.
B dinner at Badgers.
C a night at the hotel.
D lunch on the journey.

A	
B	
C	
D	

9 Why is it interesting for them to go to this particular exhibition?

A They sell video equipment.
B It gives them a chance to travel.
C There is a new computer on display.
D They can eat expensive meals.

A	
B	
C	
D	

THIRD PART

For each of the questions 1—4 put a tick (✓) in one of the boxes A, B, C or D.

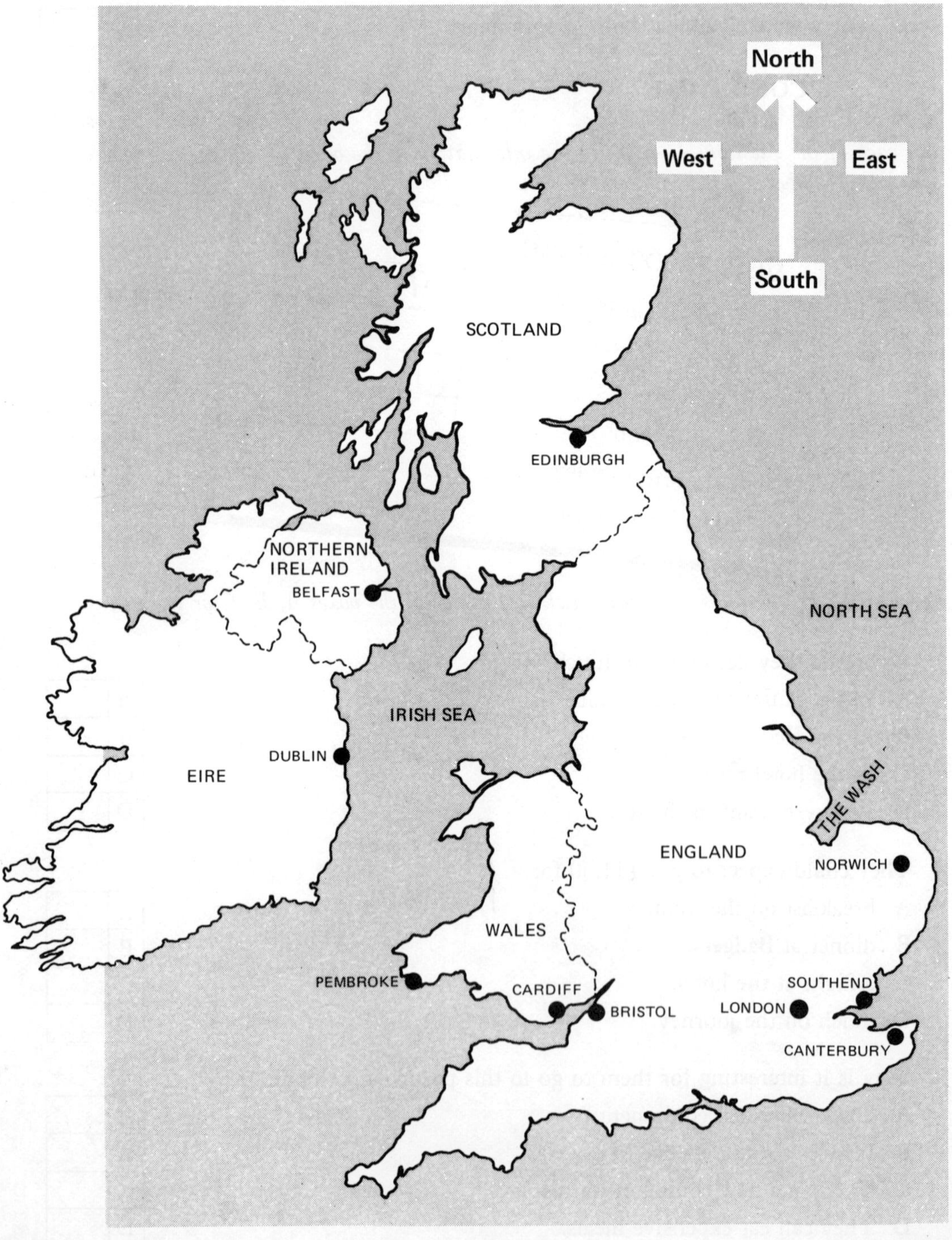

1 According to the forecast which town in the east will have hazy sunshine?

A Norwich.
B London.
C Southend.
D Canterbury.

A	
B	
C	
D	

2 By early afternoon, along the south coast it will be

A hot and sunny.
B cloudy and warm.
C wet and cloudy.
D cold and rainy.

A	
B	
C	
D	

3 Which part of the western region will have the lowest temperature?

A Bristol.
B South-west England.
C Pembroke.
D North Wales.

A	
B	
C	
D	

4 Where in Scotland will the fog fall in the evening?

A North-east.
B North.
C North-west.
D West.

A	
B	
C	
D	

PAPER 5 INTERVIEW (Approx. 20 minutes)

(i) *Look at this picture carefully and be prepared to answer some questions about it.*

1 What can you see in the picture?
2 Describe the woman standing on the left.
3 Why do you think the fair is in the middle of a town?
4 How do you think the people feel on the big wheel?

The fun of the fair
Seasonal attractions
Entertainment in towns

(ii) *Look at this passage and be prepared to answer some questions about it and then to read it aloud.*

Now if you look at the illustration of the four different types of equipment you will see that they cannot be employed in the same way. Some, for example, Apparatus A, are suitable for most fires, except those where flammable liquids are involved, then you will need to use Apparatus B. Where there is danger of electrical equipment being affected then Apparatus C, containing carbon dioxide, should be employed.

When you go around the building I want you to notice where the various types of apparatus are sited, so that in an emergency you will immediately be able to locate the right type for that particular fire. Notice also, that each piece of apparatus carries a caution sign—make sure that you follow the instructions precisely. One final warning, make sure that there is always sufficient air to avoid inhaling fumes.

SAMPLE QUESTIONS

Where do you think this situation is taking place?
What is being referred to?
What warnings are being given, and who do you think is giving them?

Now read the passage aloud.

(iii) *There may be a variety of options offered in this section. Choose one of the following:*

a) You are a customer in a shop, the examiner is the shop assistant.

Ask about: sweaters available
choice of colours
prices
if changeable
if credit cards taken, if so, which

b) You booked some tickets for a concert by 'Altered Images' but when you go to pick them up, you discover the agency has booked for 'Original Images' who you cannot stand. The Altered Image concert is now completely sold out. You do not know what information the booking clerk has, but you speak first.

c) Prescribed texts—See Appendix.

Test Three

PAPER 1 READING COMPREHENSION (1 hour)

SECTION A

In this section you must choose the word or phrase which best completes each sentence. Indicate the letter A, B, C or D against the number of each item 1 to 25 for the word or phrase you choose. ***Give one answer only*** *to each question.*

1 It is against the .... not to wear seat belts in a car.
A rule B regulation C law D order

2 All those old houses in Church Street are being pulled ....
A away B off C in D down

3 I have just .... an account with the Great Eastern Bank.
A made B opened C entered D registered

4 There was a .... failure on the underground this morning.
A signal B direction C sign D indication

5 The fishermen were .... the sinking boat by helicopter.
A taken round B drawn off C taken off D brought up

6 I don't think those curtains .... very well with the wallpaper.
A suit B go C fit D march

7 The central heating doesn't seem to be .... properly.
A going B performing C warming D working

8 In recent years inflation has almost doubled the .... of living.
A price B expense C charge D cost

9 Johnny's parents always let him have his own ....
A will B wish C way D demand

10 He .... before I had time to tell him my name.
A rang off B put down C rang up D set down

11 I heard the news .... the radio last night.
A by B on C with D in

12 I'm afraid Mr Brown isn't in. Would you like to .... a message?
A give B leave C say D tell

13 The residents are organising a protest .... against the closing of their local hospital.
A outing B march C progress D run

14 He never takes .... in any college activities.
A part B place C shares D time

15 Our .... was delayed owing to bad weather conditions.
A airline B runway C airway D flight

16 Do you get extra pay when you work .... ?
A extensively B overtime C overactively D overlong

17 Whatever .... him buy that old car?
A obliged B forced C made D encouraged

18 All medicines should be kept out of .... of children.
A hand B touch C contact D reach

19 Everything in the sale has been .... to half price.
A reduced B decreased C diminished D lowered

20 I can never touch lobster because I'm .... to shellfish.
A sensitive B allergic C infected D sensible

21 The little boy .... into tears when he thought he was lost.
A burst B fell C broke D dripped

22 All the food in that little café is ....
A handmade B self-made C homemade D home-based

23 Please inform the college secretary if you .... your address.
A move B remove C vary D change

24 Our telephone has been .... for three weeks.
A out of line B out of touch C out of order D out of place

25 Label on bottle of medicine: It is dangerous to exceed the stated ....
A drops B measure C limit D dose

SECTION B

In this section you will find after each of the passages a number of questions or unfinished statements about the passage, each with four suggested answers or ways of finishing. You must choose the one which you think fits best. Underline the letter A, B, C or D against the number of each item, 26 to 40, for the answer you choose. ***Give one answer only*** *to each question. Read each passage right through before choosing your answers.*

FIRST PASSAGE

During the Christmas shopping rush in London, the intriguing story was reported of a tramp who, apparently through no fault of his own, found himself locked in a well-known chain store late on Christmas Eve. No doubt the store was crowded with last-minute Christmas shoppers and the staff were dead beat and longing to get home. Presumably all the proper security checks were made before the store was locked and they left to enjoy the three-day holiday untroubled by customers desperate to get last-minute Christmas presents.

However that may be, our tramp found himself alone in the store and decided to make the best of it. There was food, drink, bedding and camping equipment, of which he made good use. There must also have been television sets and radios. Though it was not reported if he took advantage of these facilities, when the shop re-opened, he was discovered in bed with a large number of empty bottles beside him. He seems to have been a man of good humour and philosophic temperament—as indeed vagrants very commonly are. Everyone else was enjoying Christmas, so he saw no good reason why he should not do the same. He submitted, cheerfully enough, to being taken away by the police. Perhaps he had had a better Christmas than usual. He was sent to prison for seven days. The judge awarded no compensation to the chain store for the food and drink our tramp had consumed. They had, in his opinion, already received valuable free publicity from the coverage the story received in the newspapers and on television. Perhaps the judge had had a good Christmas too.

26 The tramp was locked in the store

A for his mistakes.

B due to a misunderstanding.

C by accident.

D through an error of judgment.

27 The staff were 'dead beat' means they were

A half asleep.

B exhausted.

C irritable.

D forgetful.

28 What action did the tramp take? He

A looted the store.

B made himself at home.

C went to sleep for 2 days.

D had a Christmas party.

29 When the tramp was arrested, he

A laughed at the police.

B looked forward to going to prison.

C took his bottles with him.

D didn't make any fuss.

30 Why didn't the judge award compensation to the chain store?

A The tramp had stolen nothing of value.

B The store had profited by the incident.

C The tramp deserved a happy Christmas.

D The store was responsible for what happened.

SECOND PASSAGE

Extractor fans and air cleaners

Stale air, cooking odours and steam in the home are unpleasant—but the answer is not necessarily to open a window. Kitchens and bathrooms present particular ventilation problems, and in both there can be a build-up of steam.

In an enclosed bathroom, with no windows, you must, by law, have a vented extraction system. These normally work on a fixed cycle and are activated when the light is switched on.

Elsewhere, ventilation normally occurs through windows, up chimney flues and through gaps in window frames. Cold air enters at the lowest level, heats, and escapes through higher-level openings.

In making homes thermally efficient, it is possible to create further problems of stale air and unwanted steam. For comfort, a minimum number of air changes are needed per hour.

These are the desirable number of air changes needed in average conditions:

Kitchen	10—15 per hour
Bathroom, W.C.	10—15 per hour
Living areas	4—6 per hour

The simplest ventilator is the window-mounted plastic grill which revolves as a result of the difference in air pressure between the inner and outer walls of the house.

31 One of the main ventilation problems is caused by

A body odour.

B open windows.

C condensation.

D overheating.

32 You are legally obliged to have a ventilator in a bathroom without

A electric light.

B a light switch.

C air-conditioning.

D natural light.

33 It is known that cold air

A increases at lower levels.

B rises as it becomes warmer.

C is warmed at higher levels.

D does not heat at lower levels.

34 The air in toilet areas needs changing

A at least every ten hours.

B not less than ten times hourly.

C every four or five hours.

D at least fifteen times an hour.

35 The simplest way to prevent stale air is to install a ventilator which

A records the air pressure.

B is between the inner and outer walls.

C responds to air pressure.

D revolves between the window and a plastic grill.

THIRD PASSAGE

How to Win at BATTLEZONE

In this game you are in a tank and the screen shows your view of the landscape outside. You gain points by shooting enemy tanks, supertanks, missiles and saucers.

Experts gain scores of around 150,000 points at this game. To get a high score you have to destroy twenty tanks as quickly as possible. After this the supertanks, missiles and saucers appear. These are worth far more points than the ordinary tanks. (The number of tanks you have to destroy before the supertanks appear varies on different machines.)

Try to approach an enemy tank from the side or the back, so it cannot shoot at you. Then, when you get close, turn to face it, line it up in your sights and fire before it turns to shoot at you. If you miss or are too slow, quickly escape by moving out of the enemy's line of fire. You can then move around the enemy and come in from another side.

When a supertank appears, try to destroy it. Then wait safely behind an obstacle for a missile or flying saucer. The cubes are useful objects to hide behind as you can fire over them without exposing yourself to danger. The missiles will fly straight at you, but they are difficult to hit, so do not shoot at them until they are quite close. The saucers are much easier to hit, but do not chase them as you will be open to attack from enemy tanks.

36 This information refers to

A an underwater game.

B a computer game.

C a board game.

D a ball game.

37 To get a high score you must first

A capture a number of tanks.

B shoot down some explosive weapons.

C destroy some armoured vehicles.

D eliminate twenty supertanks.

38 A good plan when attacking an enemy tank is to

A move it to the side.

B get behind it.

C shoot it in the back.

D move out of its range.

39 If you hide behind the cubes during an attack you can

A fire through them.

B shoot from behind them.

C be certain of hitting your target.

D let them shoot over you.

40 You are likely to be attacked if you

A fire straight at a missile.

B hit a flying saucer.

C pursue a flying target.

D chase enemy tanks.

PAPER 2 COMPOSITION (1½ hours)

*Write **two only** of the following composition exercises. Your answers must follow exactly the instructions given, and must be of between 120 and 180 words each.*

1 An American friend has invited you to spend six weeks' holiday at his/her home in Florida. Write a letter explaining why for personal reasons you will be unable to come. You should make the beginning and the ending like those of an ordinary letter, but the address is not to be counted in the number of words.

2 You were driving along the motorway with a friend who was suddenly taken seriously ill. Describe what action you took.

3 You are a reporter on your local newspaper. An exhibition of work by local artists is being held at your town hall to raise money for sick children. Write a report on this event.

4 The advantages and disadvantages of cycling.

5 (See Appendix: Prescribed texts)

PAPER 3 USE OF ENGLISH (2 hours)

SECTION A

1 *Fill each of the numbered blanks in the following passage. Use only* **one** *word in each space.*

I am .... (1) to say that the new TV comedy, *Our Mum* is very disappointing. It's .... (2) original nor amusing. We've all .... (3) all the old .... (4) about mothers-in-law until we're sick of .... (5). I suppose there are some people who still find them .... (6), but I'm afraid I'm not .... (7) of them. Betty Browning does her .... (8) but even she can't .... (9) us believe in the character of Mrs May. George Gow, ... (10) plays Fred, gives such .... (11) unconvincing performance .... (12) we can only sympathise .... (13) Mrs May for .... (14) obliged to put .... (15) with him. I think the scriptwriter will .... (16) to make considerable changes .... (17) this series is to attract viewers, particularly .... (18) it is at the .... (19) time as *Match of the Week* .... (20) the other channel.

2 *Finish each of the following sentences in such a way that it means exactly the same as the sentence printed before it.*

EXAMPLE: 'Where are my socks?' I asked my mother.

ANSWER: I asked *my mother where my socks were.*

a) What did he say when he was stopped by the police?
Tell me ....

b) He's an only child.
He hasn't ....

c) I paid £5 each for the tickets.
The tickets ....

d) She didn't tell me where she lived.
She didn't give ....

e) You know your way about London better than I do.
I don't know ....

f) He told me to come any time I liked.
He said ....

g) Was it a monkey that bit your finger?
Was your ....

h) Would you like me to help you with the washing up?
I'll help ....

i) I like swimming better than any other sport.
Swimming is ....

j) He said he hadn't stolen the money.
He denied ....

3 *Complete the following sentences with the correct preposition or particle.*

EXAMPLE: He gets ..*up*.. at 5.00 every morning.

a) I've thrown .... all my old clothes.

b) John and Jane have broken .... their engagement.

c) I can put you .... when you come to London.

d) He has come .... from the anaesthetic at last.

e) The guide took us .... the bridge to the castle.

4 *Substitute a word or phrase with the same meaning for* light *in the following sentences.*

EXAMPLE: This suitcase is quite light.

ANSWER: This suitcase is not very *heavy*.

a) The curtains in the sitting room were light blue.

....

b) There was a light on the bedside table.

....

c) I only had a very light breakfast.

....

d) The Christmas lights were beautiful this year.

....

e) His coat was too light for the frosty weather.

....

5 *Make all the changes and additions necessary to produce, from the following eight sets of words and phrases, eight sentences which together make a complete police notice. Note carefully from the example what kind of alterations need to be made. Write each sentence in the space provided.*

EXAMPLE: This child/be missing/home/three weeks.

ANSWER: *This child has been missing from home for three weeks.*

you/see/this child?

a) ....

Tommy Wills/7/be missing/home/Thursday/Jan 6.

b) ....

He/last see/when he/leave/Broadholt School/4.00 pm/cycle home/Burns Road.

c) ....

He/normally/take/short cut/across/Broadholt Common/but that day/never/arrive/home.

d) ....

Tommy/have/short dark hair/brown eyes/and/be/about 1.20m tall.

e) ....

He/wear/dark blue jeans/grey sweater/red anorak.

f) ....

If you/think/you see/Tommy/or/have/any information/which/help/us/find him/please contact Broadholt Police 246 5719 or/ring/local police station.

g) ....

All information/treat/strict confidence.

h) ....

SECTION B

6 *Using the information given, continue each of the four paragraphs in the spaces provided. Use about 50 words for each paragraph.*

TRAVELLERS' CHEQUES AND CURRENCY.

By far the most popular way of taking money abroad is by travellers' cheques.

We can provide you with Barclays Visa Travellers' Cheques. These are simple to cash all over the world and provide a safe, secure alternative to carrying all your holiday money in cash.

Depending on where you're going, they are available in either sterling or US dollars.

In the U.S.A., many banks, in fact, have no facilities for exchanging travellers' cheques or foreign currency.

So, use our dollar travellers' cheques just like the Americans do—as cash.

You'll find you can use them in many shops, hotels, restaurants and even buses as if they were actual dollar bills.

Should you ever lose them, a quick reverse charge phone call will direct you to one of thousands of refund locations around the world and stop your holiday turning into a disaster.

Of course, you'll also need some local currency for when you first arrive.

So overleaf you'll find a simple order form for all your travellers' cheques and currency.

To make it even simpler, we can deduct the total amount from your personal cheque account or Barclaycard account automatically.

And have everything ready and waiting for you just before you leave.

BARCLAYS

Travellers' cheques are popular because ....

....

....

If you are going to the U.S.A. ....

....

....

The loss of travellers' cheques ....

....

....

To order and pay for travellers' cheques and currency ....

....

....

PAPER 4 LISTENING COMPREHENSION (Approx. 30 minutes)

FIRST PART

Fill in the information you hear on the form below. Some of it has been filled in for you.

BROWN, HOLLAND & CARPENTER
15 Hall Street
London WC2

CLAIM FOR EXPENSES:
ATTENDANCE AT COURSE

Name	Department	Position held

Type of course	Where held	Duration	Date(s)
		1 Day	10th May

	£ p	Leave Blank
Travelling expenses (~~car/bus~~/train return) From.......... To.......... Westhampton		
Accommodation inclusive bed/breakfast (Give dates/details) 9th May Crown Hotel	36.00	
Meals (alcoholic drinks not included) Give date(s), details .... 10th May - Lunch at the Tech 10th May	12.00	
Additional expenses (if any) None		
NOTE: Receipts must be attached for travelling expenses, accommodation and meals.	88.50	Total

SECOND PART

For each of the questions 1—5 put a tick (✓) in one of the boxes A, B, C or D.

1 What game is being played?

A Badminton.

B Table tennis.

C Golf.

D Tennis.

A	
B	
C	
D	

2 What is the score at the end of the fourth set?

A Three all.

B Manners leading 6—4.

C Two all.

D Fitzwilliam leading 7—5.

A	
B	
C	
D	

3 According to the commentator Manners

A is expected to win the match.

B has more stamina than Fitzwilliam.

C is unlikely to retain his title.

D has played fewer matches than Fitzwilliam.

A	
B	
C	
D	

4 In the final game Fitzwilliam

A loses his service.

B has a run of bad luck.

C loses his temper.

D has an easy win over Manners.

A	
B	
C	
D	

5 The result of the match

A causes a riot in the stands.

B is something of a surprise.

C proves unpopular with the crowd.

D is very much as expected.

A	
B	
C	
D	

THIRD PART

For each of the questions 1—4 put a tick (✓) in one of the boxes A, B, C or D.

1 What has caused the trouble on the line?

A A power cut.
B A fallen tree.
C A thunderstorm.
D A strike.

A	
B	
C	
D	

2 Which train will run as far as Eastgate?

	Kipton	Birch	Eastgate	Westchester
A	7.15	7.30	7.55	8.10
B	7.50	——	8.30	8.45
C	8.05	8.20	8.45	9.00
D	8.20	8.35	9.00	9.15

A	
B	
C	
D	

3 How long will the coach take from Eastgate to Westchester?

A 30 minutes.
B 25 minutes.
C 35 minutes.
D 20 minutes.

A	
B	
C	
D	

4 Passengers wanting further information should

A telephone British Rail.
B enquire at their local station.
C listen for further information.
D contact the radio station.

A	
B	
C	
D	

FOURTH PART

Put a tick, as shown in No.1, against each object needed to make photographic prints.

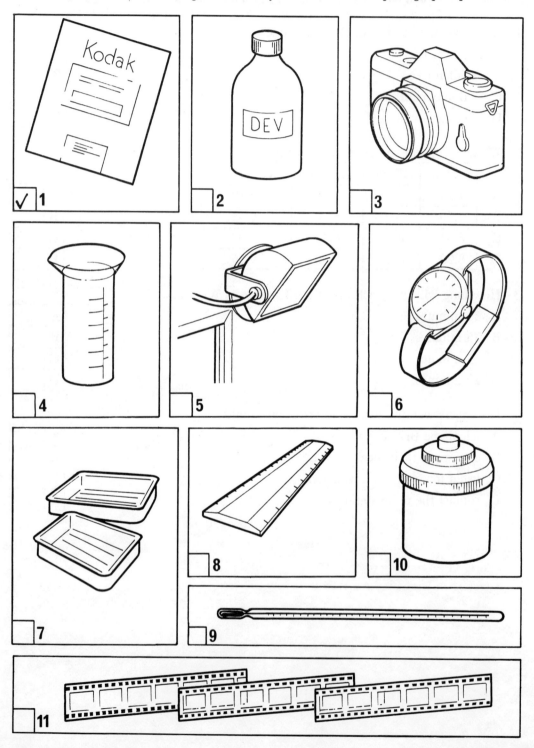

✓ 1

2

3

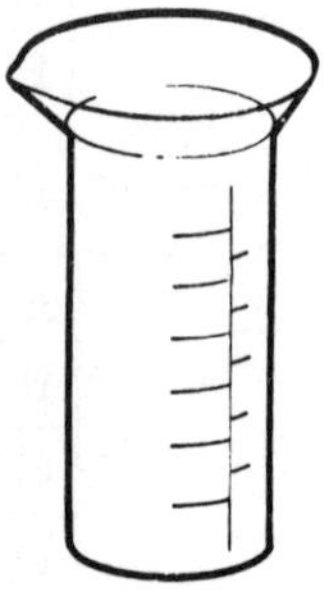

4

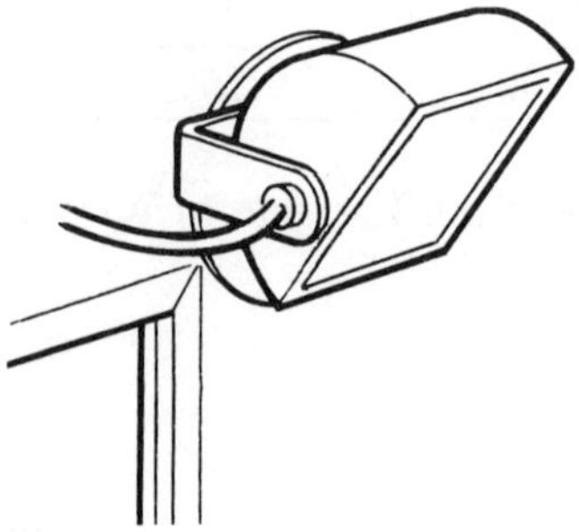

5

6

7

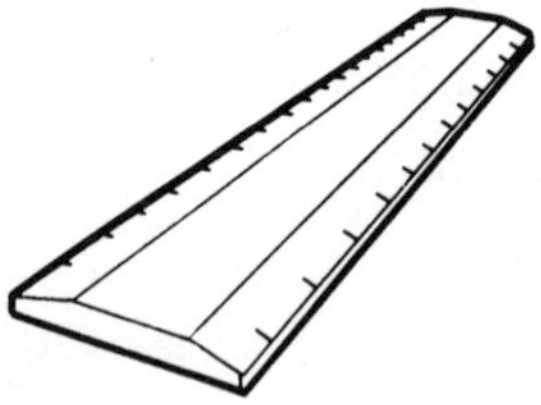

8

10

9

11

PAPER 5 INTERVIEW (Approx. 20 minutes)

(i) *Look at this picture carefully and be prepared to answer some questions about it.*

1 What is happening in the picture?
2 Describe what the men are wearing.
3 Why would this particular kind of fire be dangerous?
4 What do you think the things in the background are?

Firemen and firefighting
Importance of dangerous jobs
Danger of inflammable material in towns

in danger
must have been-past.
must be present
are in vein.
reward - [illegible]

(ii) *Look at this passage and be prepared to answer some questions about it and then to read it aloud.*

If the annual mileage is low, the following operations should be carried out.

Once a year you should: drain and refill the car engine and gearbox; remove the rear brake pads for inspection.

Every two years it is advisable to replace the hydraulic system fluid or brake fluid.

At the owner's request, a complete electronic check can also be carried out.

Before any long journey, we recommend that you carry out the routine checks listed on the checklist on the back cover of your instruction manual.

SAMPLE QUESTIONS

What is this passage about?
Who are the instructions meant for?
What checks ought to be made annually?
What should you do before going on a long journey?

Now read the passage aloud.

(iii) *There may be a variety of options offered in this section. Choose one of the following:*

a) A member of your family is seriously ill. You have to fly home immediately. Go to the airline and explain the situation.
The examiner is the airline clerk.

Ask about: times of flights
seats available
check-in times, etc.

b) Look at the picture opposite. What mistakes can you find in it?

c) Prescribed texts—See Appendix.

HARDWARE SHOP
LITTER

Test Four

PAPER 1 READING COMPREHENSION (1 hour)

SECTION A

In this section you must choose the word or phrase which best completes each sentence. Indicate the letter A, B, C or D against the number of each item 1 to 25 for the word or phrase you choose. ***Give one answer only*** *to each question.*

1 The judge gave the gangster the severest .... allowed.
A trial B sentence C defence D counsel

2 She was extremely .... , always ready to agree with other people's wishes.
A adaptable B mellow C moderate D supple

3 It was cold enough for a fire so her husband went off to .... some wood.
A crumble B splinter C chip D chop

4 The boss's ill temper in the morning was the cause of much .... in the office.
A abrasion B brittleness C friction D restriction

5 The boys pumped their beachball up too high and made it too ....
A elastic B bouncy C stretchy D flexible

6 He was extremely angry and suddenly ....
A blew off B blew out C blew up D blew away

7 The woman tripped over the uneven pavement and .... her elbow.
A dislocated B distorted C dislodged D disabled

8 He knew he couldn't change anything so he just .... himself to the situation.
A assigned B resigned C aligned D maligned

9 The weather was beautiful and the park was full of people out for a ....
A amble B wander C stroll D strut

10 There was an accident on the A40 this morning and .... there has been a severe congestion of traffic.
A until then B since then C for which D after that

11 The games table was described as a beautiful .... of furniture.
A piece B object C thing D manufacture

12 His father had been the .... of the company in 1955.
A inventor B producer C founder D originator

13 You very rarely find peas in .... nowadays, they are usually sold in packets or tins.
A shells B pods C husks D skins

14 I'm afraid I haven't got time to .... the matter right now.
A go into B look for C turn over D clean out

15 After the accident she suffered brain .... and couldn't speak.
A destruction B disease C decay D damage

16 By arriving late for the interview, he .... his chances of getting the job.
A threw off B threw away C threw down D threw over

17 .... of the two football teams scored a goal, so the final result was a draw.
A No one B None C Neither D Not any

18 In order to .... rising production costs, the subscription rates have been increased.
A tie in with B mark out from C be similar to D keep up with

19 Game pie was a .... of the restaurant.
A singularity B particularity C speciality D originality

20 Railway steam engines are a .... sight nowadays.
A rare B scarce C scant D spare

21 The children .... around the teacher as she explained something.
A united B joined C converged D clustered

22 We learnt a lot of vocabulary .... the course of the lesson.
A with B during C between D inside

23 Mr Brown was acting very peculiarly and seemed in a funny ....
A state of affairs B state of mind C state of grace D state of nature

24 The patient's progress was very encouraging as he could .... get out of bed without help.
A nearly B only C merely D barely

25 The scientists became very excited as they felt they were .... of a discovery.
A on the crest B on the surface C on the brink D on the borderline

SECTION B

In this section you will find after each of the passages a number of questions or unfinished statements about the passage, each with four suggested answers or ways of finishing. You must choose the one which you think fits best. Underline the letter A, B, C or D against the number of each item, 26 to 40, for the answer you choose. ***Give one answer only*** *to each question. Read each passage right through before choosing your answers.*

FIRST PASSAGE

There are over 250 independent hospital radio stations in the United Kingdom and they serve about three-quarters of the UK hospitals. Recently a survey was carried out on a random sample of these stations concerning their staffing, broadcasts and finance. Three hospitals also contributed information about the listening habits of almost 200 patients. The findings have been of great assistance to the people involved in patient services and have stimulated them to think critically about the radio facilities provided by the hospitals.

To obtain information about the hospital radio stations, 30 hospital broadcasting organisations were randomly selected and questionnaires were sent out. Twenty-four (80%) were returned completed. From the replies it was found that an 'average' station serves three hospitals and involves 33 people in the preparation and broadcasting of programmes. Broadcasts are put out for about 28 hours a week, mainly in the evenings and at weekends. Only 17% and 21% being broadcast in the mornings and afternoons respectively. All the stations used ward visiting to obtain record requests and many publicised their services by other means as well, for example posters, inserts in patients' guides and through local newspapers. Only 13% of the radio stations got a financial grant from the hospitals, although additional funding from voluntary organisations such as the hospitals' League of Friends goes to another 21%. The cost of a radio station to the hospital is therefore difficult to estimate, but various hospital administrators gave it as varying between £25—£2,000 per annum.

In the survey of hospital patients, it was found that of the 196 interviewed, only 22 had listened to the hospital radio service since admission. One of the main reasons given for not listening was that although 50% of the patients knew about the service only 9% knew the name of the station and how to receive it. Of these, only 3% were aware that their friends and relatives could send a get-well message or record dedication through the radio service. Another main cause of the low utilisation of the service was the unserviceability of the bedside radio headsets. Of the 22 patients who had listened to the hospital station, ten said the reception was bad, five fair, and only seven said it was good. When asked if they would listen if the reception was better, 75% of the patients who never listened said they would do so. The most popular programmes were found to be based on hospital/ward information and news, and health education; record requests came third.

From this survey it was concluded that hospital radio stations needed higher financial support to extend their services, and, most importantly, a better maintenance of the bedside radio headsets should be provided to improve reception of the broadcasts.

26 According to the passage, a survey was carried out on

A three-quarters of the patients in three hospitals.

B patients selected from 250 hospitals.

C about 200 patients in some of the hospitals.

D patients from three-quarters of the UK hospitals.

27 The completed questionnaires were important as they

A showed what kind of programmes were being broadcast.

B helped the organisers to consider future radio broadcasts.

C suggested the wrong kind of programmes were being broadcast.

D proved that the broadcasting stations were understaffed.

28 The most popular method of advertising the radio stations' services is

A through hospital publications.

B using the local press facilities.

C approaching the patients personally.

D putting up posters in the wards.

29 Almost a quarter of the radio stations received finance from

A hospital board grants.

B various voluntary bodies.

C the hospital administrators' estimates.

D a variety of other sources.

30 Many of the hospital patients did not listen to the hospital radio because

A they were unable to receive it on their bedside headsets.

B their friends and relatives did not use the radio to send messages.

C they didn't know how to tune their radios.

D they did not know the names of the programmes being broadcast.

31 Three-quarters of the patients interviewed about the radio service wanted

A technical improvements.

B more factual programmes.

C fewer record requests.

D increased medical information.

SECOND PASSAGE

A theatrical company was once performing a well-known thriller on the outskirts of London. This company had been assembled by a wealthy woman who had no experience of the stage, but whose fortune allowed her to indulge herself. The final act of this play included a small, but vital part—that of the detective. He was supposed to land by helicopter, enter through the french windows and question everyone on the stage about the murder which had taken place.

When the actor cast as the detective failed to show up for rehearsals the stage carpenter volunteered to take his place. He assured his wealthy patron that he had wide experience of comedy and that this part would be easy for him. She believed him. The rest of the company were not so sure. For some reason the carpenter only rehearsed the part once. Even so the 'manager' felt totally confident about him.

On the opening night all went well until the moment when the helicopter was supposed to land. The terrible noise from the room above, which should have set the chandelier swinging wildly and at which one of the actors was supposed to say, 'What is that awful noise?' never happened. Since the next part of the play was concerned with the noise, the actors had to do the best they could and make up the lines.

This went on for several minutes, with the cast becoming increasingly desperate when, suddenly, the chandelier began swinging violently, but in total silence. Finally the sound of the approaching helicopter was heard and the cast turned with relief to greet the detective as he entered through the french windows. The sight that met their eyes left them speechless. There stood the carpenter, dressed in a policeman's uniform but wearing enough make-up for a circus clown. He had two bright red spots on his cheeks and his lips were a vivid pink. His eyes were ringed with enormous bright blue circles, with a blob of black mascara on the end of each lash.

After delivering his first line, he then completely forgot the rest of his part. So, striding to the centre of the stage, he took off his helmet, in which he had hidden a dirty piece of paper on which he had written his lines. He started reading these like a commentator giving the racing results. When he came to turn over the page, he lost his place, fumbled hopelessly, and when he'd found it, bowed to the audience, saying 'Pardon me,' before carrying on.

He stuck to carpentry after that.

32 The owner of the theatrical company

A was too rich to be an actress.

B had enough money to put on plays.

C was rich enough to be able to act.

D put all her money into the company.

33 Why did the wealthy 'manager' believe the carpenter could play the part of the detective?

A He said he'd had wide experience in that kind of role.

B He assured her that he found all acting very easy.

C She hadn't enough experience to know any better.

D She was experienced enough to recognise a good actor.

34 The actors became increasingly desperate

A when they could think of nothing else to say.

B when one of them asked about a noise which didn't happen.

C when the chandelier began to swing about wildly.

D when there was a terrible noise but the helicopter didn't appear.

35 Why did the cast 'become speechless'?

A They couldn't remember their lines.

B They were so amazed at the carpenter's appearance.

C They were surprised the carpenter was wearing a uniform.

D They had no breath left after making up lines.

36 The carpenter decided not to act again because

A he didn't like wearing make-up.

B he realised he was more talented backstage.

C he preferred giving racing commentaries.

D he found he was too polite for the audience.

THIRD PASSAGE

●MR BROWN Tall, attractive man, single, aged 30. Outdoor type, sports-loving. Plays football, tennis and squash. Enjoys swimming and skiing. Beer drinker. PE instructor at boys' school.

●MR GREEN Unemployed, unmarried, undernourished English Lit. graduate, aged 23. Indoor type, plays 'Dungeons and Dragons' and any other role-playing adventure game. Enjoys rock and jazz records and sci-fi films and books. Lives in London.

●MR BLACK Mature man of 50, recently widowed with one son of 15. Own business and home. Enjoys bridge, French food and good claret. Very sociable, likes entertaining and travel. City dweller.

●MR WHITE Quiet, shy, peace-loving man, aged 35. Divorced, non-smoker. Ecologist, lives and works in the country. Enjoys chess, walking and reading. Likes eighteenth-century classical music and dry white wine. Dislikes noise and energetic sports.

37 What kind of publication might these people advertise in?

A A quality daily newspaper.

B A business magazine.

C A popular weekly magazine.

D A trade journal.

38 Which one would most probably appeal to a young woman of 25 who doesn't like living in town and who enjoys playing sports?

A Mr Brown.

B Mr Black.

C Mr Green.

D Mr White.

39 Mr Black is most likely to be attracted to

A an attractive widow who is very shy.

B a fun-loving, intelligent woman.

C a pretty woman who hates travelling.

D a businesswoman who is a strict vegetarian.

40 Which of these women students would probably find Mr Green interesting?

A A law student who is very logical and practical.

B A dreamy, romantic music student who dislikes pop music.

C An energetic, sociology student, interested in politics.

D An amusing, carefree art student who is very easy-going.

PAPER 2 COMPOSITION (1½ hours)

*Write **two only** of the following composition exercises. Your answers must follow exactly the instructions given, and must be of between 120 and 180 words each.*

1 You want to come to England to study English. Write a letter to an English school or college asking about courses, prices, dates, levels, etc. You should make the beginning and the ending like those of an ordinary letter, but the address is not to be counted in the number of words.

2 You have recently been to an exhibition showing what life will be like in the 21st century. Write a report on it.

3 Describe the qualities you think are necessary for a successful leader.

4 Is it possible for humans to be equal?

5 (See Appendix: Prescribed texts)

PAPER 3 USE OF ENGLISH (2 hours)

SECTION A

1 *Fill each of the numbered blanks in the following passage. Use only* **one** *word in each space.*

In today's gloomy labour market, work .... (1) to have little future .... (2) over four million unemployed. Nor does .... (3) look like a passing phase any more. The numbers .... (4) of work may stay well over three million for the .... (5) of the decade, if present government policies .... (6) unchanged. But the employment picture to the .... (7) of the century will be .... (8) from static. Indeed, Britain is already going .... (9) an occupational revolution .... (10) will transform the face of the country. The present slump has .... (11) the pace of this change. .... (12), for the first time in British history, more white-collar workers .... (13) blue-collar are in jobs. .... (14) 1990, as many as two-thirds of the total .... (15) employed will work in services and government.

Also, the rapid .... (16) of technology has led to the suggestion .... (17) over the next thirty years automation will advance with .... (18) speed that only 10% of the workforce will be .... (19) to produce material goods, the .... (20) will handle information.

2 *Finish each of the following sentences in such a way that it means exactly the same as the sentence printed before it.*

EXAMPLE: 'Don't get so excited, John,' she said.

ANSWER: She told John *not to get so excited.*

a) There weren't many people in the gallery.
The gallery ....

b) Mondays and Wednesdays are the only days he goes to college.
He only ....

c) I'm sure Carol doesn't want to go to the party.
I don't ....

d) 'How much did you pay for your new coat?' she asked.
She asked ....

e) I used to go to that restaurant every day.
That's ....

f) You'd better not disturb the workmen.
It ....

g) It's two days now since I started reading this book.
I've ....

h) Nothing I do seems to be right.
I seem ....

i) Which way's the station, please?
How ....

j) He was the sweetest little dog I'd ever seen.
I'd ....

3 *The word in capitals at the end of each of the following sentences can be used to form a word that fits suitably into the blank space. Fill each blank space in this way.*

EXAMPLE: You should be careful when using *electrical* appliances. ELECTRIC

a) He completed the report with the .... of his secretary. ASSIST

b) The .... party was to be in a week's time. ENGAGE

c) They had a most interesting .... about breakfast television. DISCUSS

d) His proposal was .... by another member of the committee. SECOND

e) Productivity has not risen very much despite massive .... EMPLOY

f) .... plates have to be developed in a darkroom. PHOTOGRAPH

g) The .... of Italy happened over 150 years ago. UNION

h) Very few countries have corporal .... in schools. PUNISH

4 *Make all the changes and additions necessary to produce, from the following eight sets of words and phrases, eight sentences which together make a complete letter. Note carefully from the example what kind of alterations need to be made. Write each sentence in the space provided.*

EXAMPLE: How/you/get on/new job?

ANSWER: *How are you getting on in your new job?*

Dear Tony,

Many thanks/your letter/arrive/yesterday.

a) ....

I/be/very sorry/hear about/your father/illness.

b) ....

be there/any chance/he come/down here/convalesce?

c) ....

As you know/there be/plenty/room/since Rupert/return/college.

d) ....

I be sure/sea air/do/your father good.

e) ....

I collect/him/station/any afternoon/next week/you put him/train.

f) ....

Let know/soon/possible/so I arrange/meet him.

g) ....

Best wishes/you/your father/us all.

h) ....

Yours,

David

SECTION B

5 *Using the following information and the graph, continue the two paragraphs in the spaces provided. Use about 100 words for each paragraph.*

... pm, 6.00.pm—11.30 pm. ...

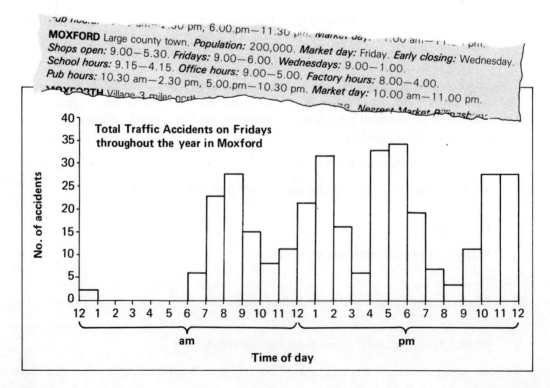

MOXFORD Large county town. *Population:* 200,000. *Market day:* Friday. *Early closing:* Wednesday. *Shops open:* 9.00—5.30. *Fridays:* 9.00—6.00. *Wednesdays:* 9.00—1.00. *School hours:* 9.15—4.15. *Office hours:* 9.00—5.00. *Factory hours:* 8.00—4.00. *Pub hours:* 10.30 am—2.30 pm, 5.00.pm—10.30 pm. *Market day:* 10.00 am—11.00 pm.

MOXFORTH Village 3 miles north ... *Nearest Market* ...

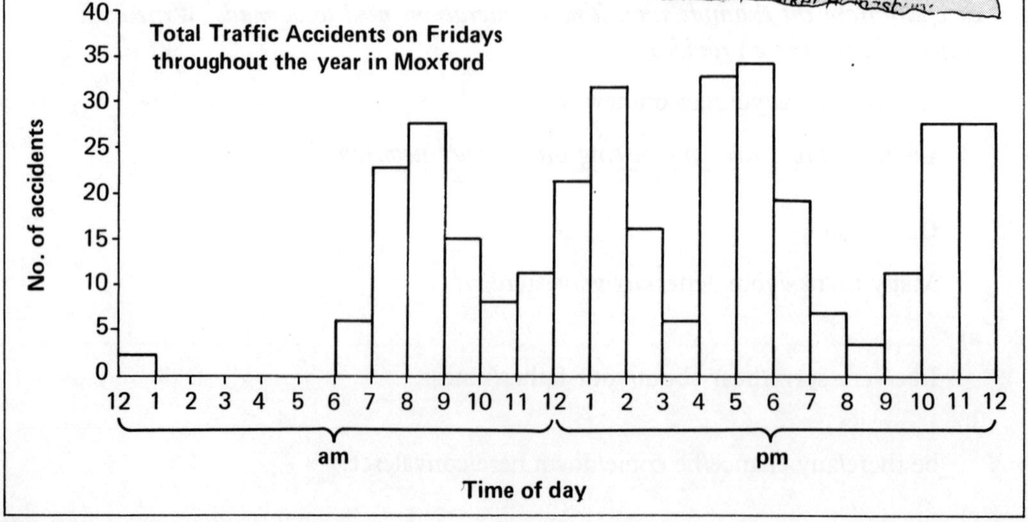

The Chief Constable of Police says there are more accidents at certain times of the day because ....

....

....

....

....

....

....

....

....

....

The Chairwoman of the Women's Institute thinks that the number of accidents on Fridays could be reduced ....

....

....

....

....

....

....

....

....

....

PAPER 4 LISTENING COMPREHENSION (Approx. 30 minutes)

FIRST PART

Fill in the information you hear on the notepad below. Some of it has been filled in for you.

Tip-Top Type Office Training

(556 8292)

Full time courses

Copy typist	8 weeks	£336	+ VAT
Audio-Typist	10 weeks	420	"
Short	12	£504	"
Shorthand + Audio Typist	14	588	"

Monday - Friday (9 – 4.30)

ADDRESS :

Edinburgh

Tel: (031) 556 8292

Check	yes	No
Start ~~any~~ on Monday?	✓	
Must pay in advance?	✗	✓
Takes credit cards?	✓	•
Interest on credit?		✓
VAT on all courses?	✓	✗

SECOND PART

For each of the questions 1—5 put a tick (✓) in one of the boxes A, B, C or D.

1 The man has gone into the car showroom

A to have a look around.

B to exchange his car.

C to look at a particular car.

D to buy another car.

A	•
B	
C	
D	

2 Why has he got to give up his motorbike?

A He has just become a father.

B His wife does not like it.

C His wife is pregnant.

D He finds it inconvenient to ride.

A	
B	
C	•
D	

3 The first car he looks at, the Fiesta,

A is rather expensive.

B is not fast enough for him.

C arrived at least a week ago.

D comes in a lot of colours.

A	x
B	•
C	
D	

4 The salesman says the Ghia

A is one of the fastest cars on the road.

B bears no comparison with the Fiesta.

C is different from most cars of the world.

D is rather over-priced.

A	x
B	•
C	
D	

5 What probably finally made the man buy a car?

A The possibility of monthly payments.

B Being able to get a reference.

C He was going to pay less than expected.

D He was tempted by it.

A	•
B	x
C	
D	

THIRD PART

Fill in the Level number you hear for the following facilities (1—9) at the Barbican Centre. No.1 has been done for you.

1	Level	4	Barbican Concert Hall
2	Level	9	Cinema 2
3	Level	1	Pit Theatre/Cinema 1
4	Level	5	Lakeside Terrace/Waterside Café/Main Entrance
5	Level	8	Art Gallery/Toilets
6	Level	2	Barbican Theatre/Toilets
7	Level	6	Conference Halls/Administration
8	Level	1	Foyer/Travel Desk/Banking/Car Parking
9	Level	7	Cut Above Restaurant/Library/Cloakroom

PAPER 5 INTERVIEW (Approx. 20 minutes)

(i) *Look at this picture carefully and be prepared to answer some questions about it.*

1 What is this man doing?
2 Describe what he is wearing.
3 What can you see lying on the ground?
4 Why do you think he is singing in the street?

Street entertainers
Begging
Alternative employment

(ii) *Look at this passage and be prepared to answer some questions about it and then to read it aloud.*

When you arrive, I want you all to stay together in case you get mixed up with other parties. You have all got your badges I hope, so please do make sure that you wear them; I don't want to have to spend half my day looking for lost lambs. Are you listening Jones? You are one of the worst offenders. Now try and practise your language as much as possible, and please, please, don't do anything silly. Now, remember the return boat leaves at 5.30 so I want to see everyone at the harbour at 5.00. That gives me time to count heads. So, off you go, enjoy yourselves and don't overeat!

SAMPLE QUESTIONS

What is happening in this passage?
Where might it be taking place?
Who is speaking to whom?
Now read the passage aloud.

(iii) *There may be a variety of options offered in this section. Choose one of the following:*

a) Think of a day last week.

Say: when you got up
what the weather was like
what you wore
where you went
mention anything unusual

b) Discuss one of the following pairs of statements.

Money is the root of all evil.	Money makes the world go round.
Good health is all-important.	The mind can overcome all things.
Life is nothing without love.	All's fair in love and war.
What is life without happiness?	Happiness is an illusion.
Life is real! Life is earnest!	Life is a toy made of glass.

c) Prescribed texts—See Appendix.

Test Five

PAPER 1 READING COMPREHENSION (1 hour)

SECTION A

In this section you must choose the word or phrase which best completes each sentence. Indicate the letter A, B, C or D against the number of each item 1 to 25 for the word or phrase you choose. ***Give one answer only*** *to each question.*

1 The headmaster has .... to improve the lighting in the school corridors.
A accepted B allowed C agreed D affirmed

2 The footballer was .... the field for kicking the referee.
A sent off B taken off C put off D brought off

3 The manager asked me if I had had any .... experience.
A earlier B before C preliminary D previous

4 .... , please. I'll see if Mr Maynard is in.
A Hang up B Hold on C Ring off D Ring up

5 What .... did you get for your English composition?
A figure B mark C number D sign

6 Please tell the children to stop .... my dog.
A trying B shocking C teasing D laughing

7 She has a very good job .... a solicitor's office.
A by B with C to D in

8 It's only a little way to the station, so we might as .... walk.
A good B well C now D quick

9 I couldn't understand what he was ....
A talking B speaking C saying D telling

10 .... about going for a swim this afternoon?
A When B Why C Who D How

11 I can't .... my mind whether to go to Switzerland or Spain for my holiday.
A make off B make up C make for D make out

12 He used to write to me regularly, but I haven't .... from him for two years now.
A received B learned C written D heard

13 It was the best holiday he had .... had.
A never B sometimes C ever D always

14 Frozen food should always be .... before it is cooked.
A melted B dissolved C defrosted D softened

15 The .... for the flat is £40 weekly.
A hire B rent C price D cost

16 I think I must have .... my wallet at home.
A forgotten B missed C taken D left

17 Is he married or .... ?
A alone B single C free D solitary

18 They .... every weekend at their cottage in the country.
A live B visit C spend D depart

19 My grandmother passed .... at the age of ninety-nine.
A out B away C off D up

20 Pop stars have to get used to people trying to get their ....
A signatures B signs C names D autographs

21 I don't know how he manages to .... his family on the small salary he earns.
A keep B retain C subsist D subsidise

22 The old man was .... asleep in his chair.
A quite B completely C well D fast

23 When you get to the High Street take the first turning .... the left.
A in B by C on D for

24 She had a lot of .... before the operation.
A pain B hurt C ache D ill

25 How does this word processor .... ?
A do B run C set D work

SECTION B

In this section you will find after each of the passages a number of questions or unfinished statements about the passage, each with four suggested answers or ways of finishing. You must choose the one which you think fits best. Underline the letter A, B, C or D against the number of each item, 26 to 40, for the answer you choose. ***Give one answer only*** *to each question. Read each passage right through before choosing your answers.*

FIRST PASSAGE

The Chelsea Gardens, when they discovered them, did not disappoint Rene's expectations. They had the grace and dignity of an English garden without the formality of a park. Arm-in-arm the two young people wandered along a path leading to a summerhouse and from there across a wide sloping lawn. Here stood a willow so ancient and whispering and curtained with leaves that it formed a giant umbrella reaching almost to the ground. Sid and Rene parted the fronds of the willow and went inside it. The sun shining through the chinks in the leaves made queer patterns on their faces. It was quiet and secret inside and Rene would have liked to sit down by the trunk. Sid looked up at the branches forming the domed roof of their hiding place, and said all those leaves were bound to be full of insects and the ground looked a bit hard here anyway. Rene gave way, not because she minded about the insects or the hardness of the ground, but because a little band of children suddenly appeared chasing one another in and out of the tree. Kids, she thought, were all right but they got in your way when you wanted to talk, and, after all, this tree must be an attraction for any kid.

'Come on,' she said, 'let's explore a bit farther.'

They went on surprisingly far to the end of the lawn, along a path and up a tiny hill till they came to a dell shaded by trees where the grass was a deeper green and velvety to the touch. It was very still here but there was no seat on which to sit down.

'It looks nice here,' said Rene, 'might as well give our legs a rest.'

Sid hesitated, torn between a desire to sit down next to Rene and the fear that he would catch a chill in the process.

'Perhaps we ought to find somewhere where there's a seat,' he suggested, 'I don't suppose the grass is dry yet after Friday's rain.'

Rene sighed. Even this velvet glade could not make Sid forget the perils associated with sitting on damp grass.

'You've got your anorak,' she said. 'You can sit on that.'

'It's my new one,' Sid began to unzip it rather half-heartedly.

'A bit of damp won't hurt it,' retorted Rene, and sat down.

26 As Rene walked through the Gardens, she found that they

A did not live up to her expectations.

B were less formal than she had imagined.

C were just as she thought they would be.

D were similar to most public gardens.

27 The willow tree on the lawn is described as 'quiet and secret' because

A it was so difficult to penetrate.

B of its dome-like shape.

C it was used as a shelter.

D its branches formed a screen.

28 When Rene suggested sitting under the tree, Sid

A made objections.

B looked uncomfortable.

C became irritable.

D seemed frightened.

29 What impression does the text give of Rene's attitude to children? She

A was very fond of them.

B had no use for them.

C sometimes found them a nuisance.

D didn't understand them.

30 From what Sid says, it seems that he

A has never sat on the grass.

B was afraid of catching cold.

C couldn't undo his anorak.

D thought it was going to rain.

SECOND PASSAGE

During the late sixteenth and early seventeenth centuries the London district of Southwark was prospering, and an extremely important and far-reaching development was taking place at Bankside, an area situated just beside the church now known as Southwark Cathedral. The Rose Theatre, the Swan, the Hope Playhouse and Bear Garden, were set up here along with the famous Globe Theatre, in which Shakespeare acted.

William Shakespeare is commemorated in Southwark Cathedral today by the modern memorial window in the south aisle. The window was designed by Christopher Webb in 1954, after an earlier window had been destroyed in the war, and depicts characters from Shakespeare's plays. Beneath it is a recumbent alabaster figure of Shakespeare, carved by Henry McCarthy in 1912, set against a background of seventeenth-century Southwark in relief, showing the Globe Theatre, Winchester Palace and the Tower of St. Saviour's Church. This memorial was provided by public subscription and was dedicated in 1911, and every year a birthday service, attended by many great actors and actresses, is held here in honour of Shakespeare's genius. Shakespeare's brother Edmund was buried here in 1607, and, although the position of Edmund's grave is unknown, he is commemorated by an inscribed stone in the paving of the choir.

31 In Shakespeare's lifetime Bankside in Southwark was notable for

A the style of its buildings.

B Shakespeare's performances at the Globe Theatre.

C its influence on public taste.

D the number of plays produced there.

32 The original memorial window to Shakespeare in Southwark Cathedral was

A designed in 1954.

B damaged by enemy action.

C replaced during the Second World War.

D carved in 1912.

33 Underneath the window there is a

A painting of seventeenth-century Southwark.

B wooden effigy.

C a sculpted figure.

D tablet dedicated to Shakespeare's brother.

34 In Southwark Cathedral, on the anniversary of Shakespeare's birth, there is

A a commemoration service.

B a drama festival.

C a special service for actors.

D a theatrical presentation.

35 This information would most likely be found in

A an advertisement.

B a historical survey.

C a tourist guide.

D a news bulletin.

THIRD PASSAGE

LANGUA·LEARN

The Natural Way to Language

CHOOSE from 30 different languages!

How did you learn to speak your language?
Did your mother give you a dictionary? Of course she didn't.
Did you have a grammar book? Of course you didn't.

YOU LISTENED, YOU UNDERSTOOD, YOU BEGAN TO SPEAK.

It's the natural way! Do it with LANGUA-LEARN.
In 4 months you'll be speaking like a native.
Astonish your friends on holiday abroad.

No more fumbling with phrase books.
No more sardines when you order lobster.

Send for our FREE DEMONSTRATION RECORD or CASSETTE and free BROCHURE.
Simply fill in the coupon below and post it to us.

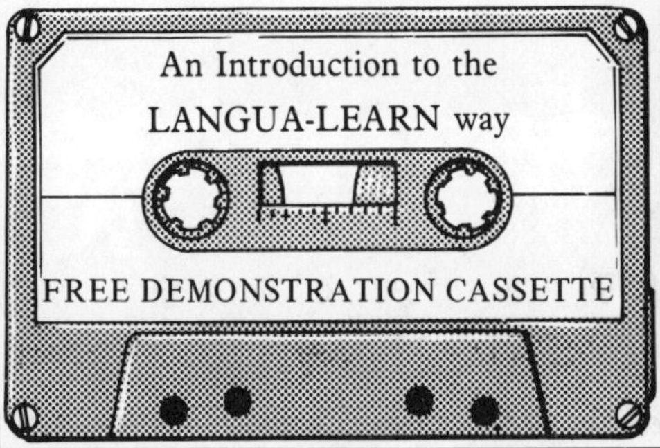

TO: Langua-Learn, Dept. 4, Cairncross Way, Epping, E5.

Name .... Age ....

Address ....

....

Language of choice .... record ☐ cassette ☐

36 The Langua-Learn course offers you a choice of

A languages spoken in 30 different countries.
B any language of your choice.
C more than 20 different languages.
D all languages other than your own.

37 According to the advertisement, you can become fluent

A without any teaching aids.
B with the minimum of effort.
C in less than a month.
D after four months' intensive study.

38 The courses advertised are mainly intended for

A homework.

B self-study.

C housework.

D private teaching.

39 The Langua-Learn method is based on the use of

A video tape.

B selected textbooks.

C recordings.

D radio programmes.

40 Further information about the course can be obtained by

A writing to the company for a form.

B attending a free lesson.

C buying a demonstration tape.

D completing a form provided.

PAPER 2 COMPOSITION (1½ hours)

*Write **two only** of the following composition exercises. Your answers must follow exactly the instructions given, and must be of between 120 and 180 words each.*

1 Write an advertisement for a job as assistant receptionist in a hotel. Give details of duties, hours of work, salary, holidays and the necessary qualifications and experience required.

2 Give your opinion about pop music.

3 How to deal with violence at football matches.

4 You are going on a camping holiday in a remote mountain area. What essential medical supplies would you take with you and say why they would be necessary.

5 (See Appendix: Prescribed texts)

PAPER 3 USE OF ENGLISH (2 hours)

SECTION A

1 *Fill each of the numbered blanks in the following passage. Use only* **one** *word in each space.*

It is extraordinary .... (1) often the telephone .... (2) when I am in the bath or in the kitchen making pastry. I never have the courage to .... (3) it ring. After all, someone might have been .... (4) to hospital, killed in an accident or .... (5) by the police. It .... (6) occurs to me that anyone would ring at .... (7) a time to give me good .... (8). So, if I'm in the bath, I jump out and run to the phone, dripping, shivering, wrapped in a towel and leaving a trail of wet footmarks .... (9) me. If I'm making pastry, it's worse, because the receiver gets covered with sticky .... (10) of flour from my hands, and the carpet looks as if it has been .... (11) out in a snowstorm. It is .... (12) consolation to hear Aunt Mary's voice asking kindly how I .... (13), or the garage ringing to say the car .... (14) now been serviced and when .... (15) I like to collect it. The only .... (16) is to leave the receiver off the .... (17), but I've tried .... (18) and it doesn't work. I mean, just supposing it was something .... (19) and I .... (20) it.

2 *Finish each of the following sentences in such a way that it means exactly the same as the sentence printed before it.*

EXAMPLE: They were mending the road all last week.

ANSWER: All last week the road *was being mended.*

a) They argued all the morning about nuclear disarmament.
They spent ....

b) Is it really necessary for you to bring all that luggage?
Do you ....

c) You shouldn't drive so fast in this wet weather.
You ought to ....

d) Vera said she would telephone me as soon as she arrived.
'I ....' said Vera.

e) Robin borrowed my dictionary last week.
I ....

f) I hadn't any change, so I couldn't telephone you.
If I'd ....

g) Do they sell fresh bread at the supermarket?
Can ....

h) Roses are my favourite flowers.
I like ....

i) The castle is said to be 500 years old.
They ....

j) What was the cause of the fire?
How ....

3 *Write in the space in each of the following sentences the correct phrase made from RUN.*

EXAMPLE: He's always *running into* debt.

a) I'm just going down to the shop to get some more sugar before we ....

b) The car skidded on the wet surface and .... the road.

c) You'll get .... if you cross the road when the traffic lights are green.

d) She .... a small hotel near Birmingham.

e) Can you .... 100 copies of this leaflet by tomorrow morning, please.

f) The little boy .... when the dog barked at him.

g) The doctor said I needed a tonic as I was rather ....

h) Shall we just .... this work first before I type it?

4 *Make all the changes and additions necessary to produce, from the following eight sets of words and phrases, a memorandum from Mary Hobson to John Pearce. Note carefully from the example what kind of alterations need to be made. Write each sentence in the space provided.*

EXAMPLE: sorry/you/unable/attend/staff meeting/15 Nov.

ANSWER: *I am sorry you were unable to attend the staff meeting on 15 November.*

FROM: Mary Hobson, Personnel Manager

TO: John Pearce, Divisional Sales Manager. 17 November, 198—

following/be/my notes/staff meeting/15 Nov/promised.

a) ....

Everyone/agree/it/be/necessary/take on/new sales rep/early spring.

b) ....

Sales/our new video games/increase/rapidly/past year/expect/go on/rise/coming year.

c) ....

I/be/anxious/have/your opinion/whether we/appoint/someone/experience/or/trainee.

d) ....

If we/appoint/trainee/then/it/be/necessary/promote/someone/your department.

e) ....

I/be/glad/have/your views/soon/possible.

f) ....

I/go/away/Dec 20/and not be/back till Jan 12.

g) ....

The matter/be/discuss/further/next meeting/Jan 20.

h) ....

SECTION B

5 *Using the information given in the following newspaper report, continue each of the four paragraphs in the spaces provided. Use about 50 words for each paragraph.*

Burlington Evening News

Residents of Burlington are being deafened by the sound of bells. Four students from Burlington College of Higher Education have barricaded themselves into the bell tower of the ancient church of St. Mary's in the High Street and have pledged themselves to ring the bells non-stop for two weeks as a protest against the heavy goods vehicles which now thunder day and night through the narrow High Street.

'They are a perpetual nuisance,' said John Norris, 18, one of the protesters. 'They not only make it difficult to sleep at night, but they are damaging our historic old houses and shops, and in particular the church, which is badly in need of restoration.'

'If we must have these juggernauts on the roads,' said Jean Lacey, biology student, 17, 'why don't they build a motorway and bypass the town? Burlington isn't much more than a large village. Its streets were never meant for heavy traffic.'

Harry Fields, 19, also studying biology, said they had decided to peal the bells as a protest. Harry said they wanted to make as much noise as possible to force the Town Council to realise just what everybody was having to put up with. 'Most of the councillors don't live in Burlington itself anyway,' he said, 'they come in for meetings and that, but the Town Hall's been soundproofed, so they probably don't notice the noise all that much, and it isn't their houses that are being damaged.'

The fourth student, Liza Vernum, said she thought the public were mostly on their side, but if they weren't, they soon would be because they wouldn't be able to stand the sound of the bells.

I asked if bell-ringing wasn't rather dangerous.

'Oh, actually,' she said, 'we're all pretty good at it. Three of us are auxiliary bell-ringers for the church anyway. John's the only one who doesn't know much about it, but he's a quick learner. Anyway, we need someone to slip out and get food and things.'

'But what about the police?' I asked her, 'aren't you afraid you'll get arrested?'

'Not really,' she said, 'we're proper bell-ringers, after all. There's no law against practising.'

I left the church with the clang of bells echoing in my ears.

The priest was not available for comment.

Meanwhile the bells continue to ring in Burlington.

The students are ringing the church bells in Burlington because...

....

....

....

....

....

Jean suggests that...

....

....

....

....

....

The Town Council are not particularly concerned..

....

....

....

....

....

Liza doesn't think the police...

....

....

....

....

....

PAPER 4 LISTENING COMPREHENSION (Approx. 30 minutes)

FIRST PART

Fill in the information you hear on the form below. Some of it has been filled in for you.

Application Form

Only available if applied for within 30 days from date of purchase.

Please complete in BLOCK CAPITALS. Detach and forward with your remittance to:
Household Insurance Services Limited
Nelson House
Upper Mayfield Road
Oxbridge
Kent

Name......M. Lewis.........

Address......27 ABBY Rd. London

....

....

....

Date of purchase

1......24 August 1983 2......Hobs......

Item

1......10 August 1982......Philiphs 2000 TV

Make

1......Rolfeat......2......Philips......

Model

1......CRESTA......2......Philips 2000......

Length of original warranty

1......1 year......2......1 YEAR

Equipment to be insured
Tick as applicable

DIS 007

Warranty extended to five years	**Premium £**
Colour television *less than 18″*	☑ B 25.00
Colour television *18″ and over*	☐ A 16.00
Video recorders	☐ C 72.00
Video cameras	☐ D 35.00
Mono television	☐ E 10.00
Hi-fi, music centres etc. *excluding styli*	
1 up to £500 value	☐ F 21.00
2 up to £1000 value	☐ G 25.00
Washing machines/washer dryers	☐ H 30.00
Spin/tumble dryers	☐ I 20.00
Refrigerators	☐ J 11.50
Freezer or fridge/freezer *excluding food spoilage cover*	☐ K 13.50
	☐ L 20.50
Freezer or fridge/freezer *including food spoilage cover*	☐ M 18.00
Microwave ovens	☐ N 30.00
Dishwashers	☐ O 18.00
Cookers *gas or electric*	☑ P 12.00
Hobs *gas or electric*	☐ Q 22.50
Double ovens *gas or electric*	☐ R 18.00
Single ovens *gas or electric*	

Warranty extended to three years	
Video recorders	☐ S 42.00
Video cameras	☐ T 15.00

How to apply
Complete the application form. Tick the box appropriate to your product(s). Detach and forward the form with your cheque or postal order to Household Insurance Services Limited at the address shown. Cheques should be made out to Household Insurance Services Limited.

A Certificate of Insurance will be sent to you and this should be kept carefully together with this leaflet and your receipt showing the date of purchase of the item(s) insured.

SECOND PART

For each of the questions 1—5 put a tick (✓) in one of the boxes A, B, C or D.

1 The Planetarium is concerned with

A charts made by astrologers.
B the study of the heavens.
C the rotation of the earth.
D maps invented by astronomers.

A	
B	
C	
D	

2 Among the exhibits at Madame Tussauds there are figures of

A people murdered there.
B missing persons.
C notorious criminals.
D people wanted by the police.

A	
B	
C	
D	

3 John doesn't want to go to Madame Tussauds because he

A thinks waxworks are silly.
B is studying zoology.
C collects pet snakes.
D is more interested in living creatures.

A	
B	
C	
D	

4 During their outing the class are going to

A have a picnic in the park.
B attend a class in the open air.
C make a cultural visit.
D work on a school project.

A	
B	
C	
D	

5 Miss Morgan gives the impression that she

A is a responsible teacher.
B likes to get her own way.
C takes no notice of the children.
D is a strict disciplinarian.

A	
B	
C	
D	

THIRD PART

Fill in the names and times of the television programmes from the information you hear.

Recor

BBC1

7.10 . . Sports . . . .

7.40 **Open All Hours.** Comedy series starring Ronnie Barker.

8.10 **Dallas**

9.00 . . News . . . .

8.50 **Kojak.** Thriller serial in six parts. Part Two.

10.30 **Match of the Day.**

11.15 **Newsnight.** Robin Day discusses today's news with 4 MPs.

CLOSEDOWN

ITV

7.00 **This is Your Life.** Who is the Celebrity Guest tonight?

7.30 . Coronation Street . . . . . .

8.00 **London Night Out.** Stars, Comedy, Top-line Entertainment.

9.00 . . Charly Chaplin . .

10.00 **News at Ten.**

10.30 . . Snuke . . . .

11.15 **Dolly Parton.** Country and Western

11.45 **Weatherman**

CLOSEDOWN

BBC REG… …EGIONS

PAPER 5 INTERVIEW (Approx. 20 minutes)

(i) *Look at this picture carefully and be prepared to answer some questions about it.*

1 Describe what you can see in the picture.
2 What kind of place is this?
3 What kind of shops can you see?
4 What are the people in the front on the left doing?

Shopping precincts
Pedestrian areas in towns
Types of shopping in modern centres

lunch – Tanaka

Wokinghams.

(ii) *Look at this passage and be prepared to answer some questions about it and then to read it aloud.*

If the baby appears to be choking, don't waste time trying to pick the object out with your fingers, unless it's easy to get hold of. Probably it will be too far back and too slippery. Hold the baby upside down by the legs. Slap the baby's back smartly between the shoulder blades. If this doesn't do the trick, do it again. If, after several tries, this hasn't worked, as a last resort give the baby's tummy a short, sharp squeeze. This should push the object out of the baby's windpipe.

SAMPLE QUESTIONS

What situation does this passage refer to?
What does it tell you not to do?
What is the first thing you should do?
What do you do if this doesn't work?

Now read the passage aloud.

(iii) *There may be a variety of options offered in this section. Choose one of the following:*

a) You are an assistant in a bookshop. A customer wants to obtain a copy of *Practical Economics* by Leonard Judson. The examiner is the customer.

Ask the customer to repeat the title and name of the book. Tell the customer it is not in stock and offer to obtain it. Say how long it will take.

Ask for the customer's name, address and telephone number. Repeat it.

Promise to advise the customer as soon as the book arrives.

b) Group or pair work—discuss:
In what order of importance you would list the following in:
A a close friend? B a bank manager?

1 sense of humour
2 generosity
3 good listener
4 kindness
5 honesty
6 understanding
7 business sense
8 patience
9 discretion
10 reliability

c) Prescribed texts—See Appendix.

Appendix: Prescribed Texts

Candidates may choose one of the questions on prescribed books as a basis for one topic in Paper 2 (Composition) and one for the Paper 5 (Interview).
The texts set for 1984 are:

JANE AUSTEN: *Sense and Sensibility*
G. B. SHAW: *Arms and the Man*
GRAHAM GREENE: *The Third Man*

Different texts may be substituted from year to year for one or all of the books prescribed.
Candidates should be reminded that only **one** of these topics can be chosen for Paper 2 (Composition). The other must be selected from topics 1—4.
Following are examples of the kind of topic the candidate may be asked to deal with on prescribed books:

SENSE AND SENSIBILITY

COMPOSITION (Paper 2)

a) Give an account of the incident that led to Marianne's first meeting with Willoughby and what followed.
b) How did Eleanor first learn of Edward's engagement to Lucy Steele? What was her reaction?
c) What do you learn from *Sense and Sensibility* of how the way of life and opportunities for young women differed from those of today?

INTERVIEW (Paper 5)

a) What explanation did Willoughby give to Eleanor for the letter he wrote to Marianne?
b) In what way are the characters of Eleanor and Marianne different?
c) Why did Colonel Brandon leave so suddenly on the morning of the excursion to Whitwell?

ARMS AND THE MAN

COMPOSITION (Paper 2)

a) Describe the incident in which Bluntschli challenges Sergius to a duel.
b) Give an account of the relationship between Sergius and Louka.
c) What impression does Bluntschli give of his attitude to war and his opinion of soldiers?

INTERVIEW (Paper 5)

a) Why did Raina call Bluntschli the 'chocolate cream soldier'?
b) How was Petkoff's old coat lost and found?
c) What advice did Nicola give to Louka about her behaviour?

THE THIRD MAN

COMPOSITION (Paper 2)

a) What was the conversation that took place between Harry Lime and Rollo Martins on The Wheel?
b) Give an account of Martins' public appearance as the famous writer, Benjamin Dexter.
c) What part does Herr Koch play in the story?

INTERVIEW (Paper 5)

a) How and where did Harry Lime die?
b) Who was Anna Schmidt? How did Martins first meet her?
c) What did Martins tell Calloway about his schooldays with Harry Lime?